Enable Me, Lord, to Shift

Are you stuck in idle? Learn how to shift into Truth and live!

Relational Domain
Book 4

By

Darlene A. Larson

Enable Me, Lord, to Shift

Author: Darlene Alene Larson
Product of Hearts with a Purpose.
www.Heartswithapurpose.com
Darlene@Heartswithapurpose.com

Author's note. I coach women. I teach women. In this book you will read some of their stories. I have changed names, locations, and situations to guard their privacy yet tell their story.

Subjects: Larson, Darlene Alene/Inspirational Coaching Devotional for Women/Spiritual Living/Christian Growth—United States.

Cover by: Taiwo David, Fiverr & Helen Blanchard

Title: *Enable Me, Lord, to Shift: Are you stuck in idle? Learn how to shift into Truth and live!* Relational Domain, book 4.

ISBN: 978-1-7335405-3-7

Printed in the United States of America

ACKNOWLEDGEMENT

This book was written with the prayers and encouragement of many loved ones. And to all of you that have prayed for me or encouraged me along the way, I say "Thank you."

I want to especially thank my Hearts with a Purpose Advisory Board for cheering me on to keep writing: Diana Luckhardt, Susan Loomis, Helen Blanchard, Debra Hinken, Jerry & Sheri Felix, Deanna Case, Linda Boyer, Ruth Ensminger, and Connie Van Houten. I could not have done this without your support.

A BIG thank you to Pastor Robert Winter for critiquing my biblical accuracy of each verse.

Thank you to my West Michigan Word Weavers writing group who read, edited, suggested, and affirmed me in my writing journey.

And lastly to my mighty Father God, I thank you and love you!

DEDICATION

I dedicate the devotional series *Enable Me, Lord, to Shift*, in memory of my parents, Allan Kaye and Donna Terrell. Being raised on the family farm in mid-Michigan, I saw my father sow seed and my mother sow love.

As I penned the devotionals, *Enable Me, Lord, to Shift*, I often reflected on farm life, which includes planting time, growth time, and harvest time. In the springtime my father would plow the fields, disc the fields, drag the fields, and again drag over the fields. This was to prepare the soil to receive the seed.

Once the seed was planted, it would take a few weeks for it to sprout. Weeds grew too. They desired to choke out the seedlings. To kill those weeds, my siblings and I hoed many fields row by row. After all, we wanted the plants to live, grow, and thrive. Then a harvest of corn, soybeans, wheat, and or sugar beets would be the profit.

My father's sowing of the seed foreshadowed to me to know how to sow the Word of God into my heart, one verse at a time. It would take me time to grow. Plus, I needed to beware of the weeds that spring up from life.

My heart's desire for my readers is to receive the seed of Truth into your heart so that you might grow in freedom, experience your life purpose, and produce a harvest gleaned from your life.

INTRODUCTION

When I picture the word shift, I think of my first driving lessons. Like many other baby boomers, I was taught to drive with a stick shift. My dad's red Ford pickup was equipped with a stick shift—a long, skinny metal stick with a knob on top that came up from the floor board. The stick danced as you drove down the road. When I was driving, it was positioned to the side of my right leg.

In newer pickups, the gear shift was a lever located behind the steering wheel. The driver had to visualize the letter H to know how to shift. First gear was at the top left of the H. Second gear was at the bottom left of the H. Third gear was at the top right of the H, and reverse was at the bottom right of the H. If you never learned to feel for the gentle nuances between the clutch and the brake, the truck would jolt and jerk, and you wouldn't get far. And if you shoved the "stick shift" to the middle of the H, you went nowhere, even though the engine kept on running. That's called idling.

Later on in life, I'd discover that learning to shift that old truck would be a lot like my journey through life. Like many women, I'd be tempted to remain stuck or push my way through the gears without learning the rhythms of the engine. My spiritual life would sputter, stall, and get stuck in idle. Isn't that a bit like so many women's lives? We run, but do we get where we want to go?

Women's lives are full. Media feeds us false messages of who we should be. The fast pace of life leaves us harried and exhausted. Social media tempts us to compare ourselves with women in our church, community, across the nation, and even around the world. We frantically scour the web, television, or shopping aisles searching for peace neatly wrapped in pleasure. In our efforts to run through life, we grind our gears and idle in agitation. We need to shift into another gear—a life of freedom.

Enable Me, Lord, to Shift is a series of inspirational coaching devotionals that teaches readers to examine every domain of their lives. In order to change, we must look at who we are and then evaluate our life. We must embrace the good but also pull up the dead weeds in order to plant the seeds of Truth that bring about spiritual transformation and wholeness. The Truth is vitally important, and that's why I capitalize it through this book. Transformation takes time and practice. Only you can change yourself. I know because I learned these principles through the discipline of pain and personal practice. I invested my time, and the seeds that were planted years ago have multiplied.

I coach women. I teach women. In this book you will read some of their stories. I have changed some of the names, locations, and situations to g*uard their privacy yet truthfully tell their stories.*

A reminder, I am not a counselor or a therapist, I am a coach. If you sense you need to talk to a counselor go, do not linger.

Enable Me, Lord, to Shift, offers you a self-assessment report card, a verse, an inspiring story, and coaching questions to help you evaluate your life and align it with the Truth of God's Word. This book will teach you how to shift from being stuck—to the Truth in order to live a life of freedom and walk in your true identity within your relationships and experiences.

I encourage you to grab your Bible and read each verse for yourself. This encourages the habit of opening the Word and personalizing the Truth. Then if you desire, mark, highlight, or underline each verse so you can easily find it again to refresh and revitalize your spirit. Read the inspirational story, answer the questions, and close with the prayer.

Are you ready to make the shift? If so, the best time to begin is **now.**

BIG PICTURE ASSESSMENT

You will discover a BIG picture quick assessment in each devotional of the *Enable Me, Lord, to Shift* series. After you complete this book and the assessment, if you choose to purchase another *Enable Me, Lord, to Shift* book, you will be able to compare your growth.

In order to know where to head, we must assess our current status. We each are Queen of our own personhood, and God gives us free will. We run our life from several domains each day. A domain is a territory over which dominion is exercised, and you are the Queen of yours.

According to Merriam-Webster online dictionary, synonyms for the word domain include area, arena, department, field, Kingdom, precinct, province, realm, specialty, sphere, or terrain. Circle the word(s) that you relate to. This book will focus on your growth in your relational domain.

First, please date your BIG picture assessment on page 11. Now, grab some crayons or markers for the coloring assessment exercise. Please do not over-think this page. Keep it simple. Look at each domain, segment, or piece, and quickly color or shade in how positively you believe you are performing in that domain. More color means you are doing well. Less color means you are not doing as well. Start at the bottom of each section and color up. For example, your relationship with the Lord is in the spiritual arena. Color in how much you believe you are in sync with God's Word.

The mental domain represents your thought life. Is it healthy? Balanced? Positive? Wholesome? Or are your thoughts negative and critical most of the time?

Your emotions are your feelings. Do you control them or do your feelings run you?

The relational domain encompasses your relationships. How are you handling them? Is any toxicity growing in your life? Do you react or respond to people?

The physical domain represents how you take care of your body and your surroundings.

The financial domain represents your finances. This includes your budget, tithe, savings, giving, and spending. How healthy are your finances?

The vocational domain includes your current career and life purpose. Are you living in your sweet spot? Do you know your passion, purpose, and calling, and are you investing in those areas? Quickly color in each area.

Great job!

Now list in order the domains that you need to work on by looking at the colored sections with the least amount of shading. Remember, this is where you are *today*. If you notice anything else you think is important on this page, please jot that down.

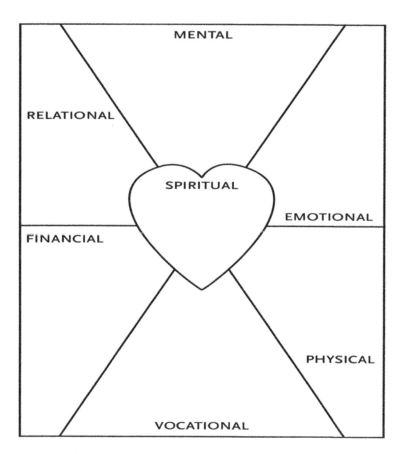

Date of assessment:_____

List in order of importance the domains you feel you need to work on:
1. _____
2. _____
3. _____
4. _____
5. _____
6. _____
7. _____

What new insight did you glean?

Welcome to book number four of the *Enable Me, Lord, to Shift* series: *Are you stuck in idle? Learn how to shift into Truth and live* is about the relationship domain of your life. Read, take an inventory of your life domains, and grade yourself with a self-assessment report card that evaluates your relationships. Then answer the coaching questions, apply the verse, and grow in your relationships.

We long, desire, want, and hunger for relationships. We strive to connect. Bond. Link. Share. Associate. Yet life brings us no certainty when it comes to people. Humans have free will. Only you can control you and change you, and only I can control me and change me. So what will we choose?

1. Choose to grow and learn to love well in relationships through Christ's enabling and everlasting love.

2. Or choose to be self-sufficient, selfish and deny His help.

Which do you choose? Circle the number.

If we do not invite Christ's Word into our heart (mind/volition), then skewed, sin-filled thoughts dominate our decisions, and a domino effect of destructive decisions decimate our relationships. Our thinking becomes all about me. Pride and self-sufficiency slither in and selfish thoughts and actions multiply.

Our lies pile up: *It's all about me. I will not trust. I will not put my heart out there. Withdraw. Hide. If I don't take care of me, who will? Besides, I'm not good enough. Bad. Loser. Worthless. Jealous. Greedy. I'm a failure. My life doesn't matter. I have nothing to offer. I can't and I will never change. Plus it is your fault.*

Our lies spin on and on, weaving a web of deception and destruction that sabotage our relationships: anxiety, anger, abuse, addictions, and/ or passive-aggressive behavior that incites divisions, disasters, divorce, and sometimes suicide.

The enemy rejoices. Separates human beings. Isolates. He gets us on our backs like sheep. Stuck. Sick. Legs straight up in the air. If you are waging war with believing lies, I suggest that when you finish this book you read Book Number 2 of the *Enable Me, Lord, to Shift* series as it addresses our thought lives.

Each of us is created in the image of the Holy God. Relationships are integral to Our Heavenly Father. Daily He is in relationship with His Son and the Holy Spirit. They are three in one. All three are equal and powerful as the Trinity: God the Father, Jesus the Son, and the Holy Spirit. These three not only enjoy the *only* perfect, consistent, loving relationship in existence day in and day out; God the Father, Son, and Spirit share an *eternal* perfect, consistent, loving relationship. And we are God's image bearers; therefore, we long for connection and conversation and to be known for our True identity as our relational God created us. If we have a personal relationship with the Lord—meaning that we've recognized that we are sinners and in need of a Savior and have prayed to receive Him as our Lord and Savior—the Holy Spirit Himself lives within us and seals us until we meet the Lord either through death or His second coming.

Back to our free will. We choose how we behave. When it comes to relationships, we must examine our heart and actions. Someday we will bow before Father God and be held accountable for our behavior. May that thought cause us to be serious about changing—relationships are His gifts to us.

If you have not read books 1, 2, or 3 of the *Enable Me, Lord, to Shift* series, I suggest you read them. They will enhance your transformational growth.

Book #1, the red book, covers the spiritual domain or growth in your relationship with the Lord and reminding you that your life matters.

Book #2, the blue book, teaches the reader how to grow Truthful thoughts in their mind.

Book #3, the brown book, teaches the reader how to guide her feelings to bow to the Truth, the Word of God. Each book teaches the reader how to apply one verse at a time.

This book, #4 of the series, offers readers a devotional and a verse a day, three coaching questions, and closes with a prayer. This book helps the reader grow in her relationship domain.

The more we graze and gaze into the mirror of Truth, the Bible, the more we fall in love with the author of our life, God. This creates a hunger to obey our Father and to choose change. This change is not a short-cut or quick fix. It's the kind of change that breaks our hearts and molds us as the Word percolates throughout our spirit, soul, and body. It spills over, delivering us from stubborn, sin-filled-strongholds and giving life-giving transformation that impacts our relationships.

So what must we change?

1. A person can choose to live according to the God-breathed inspired principles of the Word.
2. A person can throw away the Word of God, believing it offers nothing in the way of relevant material to do life and/or relationships.
3. A person can pick and choose which verses to follow or not. But they'll still fall down on their backside. *All* of God's Word is inspired. Not just certain verses. It is Truth as He is Truth. Real and relevant for a woman, even for such a time as this.

I choose to live by which number? _____.

So what do healthy relationships look like? How do they work?

James 3:13-18 states, "Who among you is wise and understanding? Let him show by his good behavior his deeds in the gentleness of wisdom. But if you have bitter jealousy and selfish ambition in your heart, do not be arrogant and *so* lie against the truth. This wisdom is not that which comes down from above, but is earthly, natural, and demonic. For where jealousy and selfish ambition exist, there is disorder and every evil thing. But the wisdom from above is first pure, then peaceable, gentle, reasonable, full of mercy and good fruits, unwavering, without hypocrisy. And the seed whose fruit is righteousness is sown in peace by those who make peace" (NASB).

Our behavior models what is *at and in* the well-spring of our heart. If it's the golden god of self, *it's all about me. My wants* or my selfies will dangle from my relationship tree. Do selfies hang from your relationship tree? If so, what is it you want to receive from others? What is your unmet need? It's crucial to get to the root and pull that out. Fill it with Jesus' love. That love never runs out. Only as you are filled with Jesus love will you experience healthier relationships.

Here are a few ingredients God wants in our relationships.

Gentleness	Kindness
Wisdom	Goodness
Purity	Love

Peace	Self-control
Reasonableness - willing to yield	Compassion
Mercy	Truth
Steadfastness, stability	Humility
Integrity - without hypocrisy	Undivided Heart
Righteousness	Repentance
Patience	Thankfulness

If you are genuinely walking in the power of the Holy Spirit, you will be reflecting the qualities of the *first list*. If we choose not to do relationships God's way, we will produce earthly, natural, rotten, and even demonic fruit. It's like we are a willing participant in the enemy's plan. If you relate more on this second list then you already have allied yourself with the agenda of Satan.

Bitterness	Greedy
Jealousy	Impatient
Selfishness	Abusive
Ambitious for oneself	Manipulative
Arrogant	Gossiping
Deceptive	Fearful
Liar	Fickle
Anxious	Stubborn
Chaotic	Proud
Evil	Opposed the Lord

Which list are you primarily living by?

Go to the list of God's way which produces peace, joy, love, and fulfillment.
Circle the attributes you are pursuing now. Great job!
Now highlight the ones you want more of and will start pursuing in your relationships.

You will start stepping out to this by_____(date).

Now go to the natural and demonic list, circle what you do (if you do any). Highlight the ones you want to starve out of your life. Put a #1 by the one you will starve out first by asking for God's help. You will start this on _____ (date).

The goal with the relationship devotional is to take the Word of God and apply each day's verse. This will enable us to shift our thinking and actions in order to develop, enhance, and grow in healthier relationships. Let's dig in and check where we're at in this domain of our life.

RELATIONAL DOMAIN REPORT CARD

We are familiar with school and certification grading systems that measure our achievement and grasp of various areas. Likewise, this report card provides a snapshot of your current status in the relational domain of your life. The report card is provided to encourage and empower you. This tool allows you to see what clutters up your life and/or stops you from reaching healthy relationships. Based on this knowledge, you can create steps to close those gaps. Take time with the report card. Enjoy the process. Allow yourself to be you, and don't be too hard on yourself or too easy. We take baby steps toward change. The little steps we take are the ones that tend to stick in life. You can do this, and I am praying for you.
Today's date_____.

- ♥ Give yourself a current over-all grade for the relational domain of your life.
- ♥ Will you allow God access to your life with your relationships?
- ♥ What would you like your relationship domain grade to be after you complete the 31-day relational domain devotional?

This book will come to life, *if* you apply the Word to your life and walk out the power of the verses.

1. What do you currently like about your relationships?

2. What do you not like about your relationships?

3. I will choose to address (this issue), #2) within _____ days.

4. I want more of (circle the ones you desire) joy, talking, walking together, listening, being positive, not reacting, less anger, speaking truthfully about my feelings, praying together, openess, not withholding, engaging, less TV, less sports, more intentional conversation with loved ones and/or ...

5. I want (#4) _____ by 6 months.

6. I will stop (#2) _____

and work toward (#4) _____

7. I will tell a friend what I am doing by _____

Draw a visual of yourself and how you want to engage in relationships. What do you see yourself doing, living, being, walking out? Draw what you see and desire for developing healthy relationships, even if you're at the beginning of the process.

If I am a believer, a Christian, I recognize this Truth and am willing to sign this report card to reinforce that I believe in the transforming power of the Holy Spirit. I choose to die to my old ways and to grow as I obey what Jesus says.

"But the Helper, the Holy Spirit, whom the Father will send in My name, He will teach you all things, and bring to your remembrance all that I said to you" (John 14:26 NASB).

Sign your name:_____

Friend/ or coach's signature to hold you accountable:

_____

My closing pep-talk words to you: take heart, each human is created in the image of God. No one is better. No one is less-than. Each has a soul. Each is a sinner. Each person has different genes, which crave to be explored. To be known. We all long to live, laugh, love, receive love and linger on God's earth while making an impact. And only through relationships can we leave a lasting legacy. Reflect now and praise Him for the people who have crossed your path and made it richer for the meeting. Write down their names.

A few of mine are: Kaye, Donna, Allan, Janice, Chris, Jill, Mia, Jeremy, Siena, Cindy, Sheri, Jerry, Bill, Helen, Alan, Lisa, Jeff, Susan, Jason, Hunter, Josh, Deb, Diana, Bill, Tammy, Deanna, Mark, Natalie, Merrily, Jon, Anastasia, Elliott, Derek, Huntley, Emma, Janaya, Joel, Ruth, Pat, and many more. Thankful. Relationships. Gifts. Love. Not to be used, cast off, or thrown aside. Only people go to heaven, not things, money, or techy tools. Let's invest in our relational domain to impact our relationships.

RELATIONAL DOMAIN DEVOTIONALS

Enable Me, Lord, to Shift
from not knowing how to treat people —
to *treating people the same way we want them to treat us.*

DAY 1

*In everything, therefore, treat people the same way you want
them to treat you...* (Matthew 7:12a NASB)

There is something healthy and simple about being raised on a farm and in community among people that turn over the soil for a living and work the land. It's as if working with dirt and seeds gives a passage of acceptance to others—we're *all* on a growth journey. We all participate in a process. And my parents, far from perfect, were ordinary farmers who didn't want to be perceived as anything other than farmers. No hypocrisy. They were my foundational role models who lived by the golden rule, "In everything, therefore, treat people the same way you want them to treat you..." (Matthew 7:12a NASB).

Knock on our farmhouse door and my mom would've invited you in and immediately asked, *How are you?* It didn't matter if you were rich, poor, in-between, family member or not, neighbor or stranger, you were given a spot at our dining room table. Sit and sip coffee, hot tea, or water, and sample homemade cookies or her famous cinnamon rolls. And if she had only one piece of pie, she gave it away. "In everything, therefore, treat people the same way you want them to treat you..."

My father taught us if we grabbed a hoe from the barn, borrowed a bike from our sibling, or a cup of sugar from the neighbor, we first asked permission. Then we were to return it to the exact location we took it from and in the condition it was in when we borrowed it when we were done. "In everything, therefore, treat people the same way you want them to treat you..."

21

How do you apply this verse on the farm or off the farm? I suggest we start with ourselves. Go look in the mirror and answer the question, *How do you want to be treated*? Write down your answer—5 desires at least.

1.

2.

3.

4.

5.

Deliver that to others.

I offer a word of warning. If you are living with a narcissist and/or are involved in toxic relationships, toxic people do life from another source. Their goal in life is *all* about themselves. If you apply the golden rule in an abusive relationship and your heart feels as if it's been raped and a thermometer of resentment shoots up inside you, set boundaries. You're being used. Guard your heart and seek counsel.

So how should we treat safe people? Recognize them. Acknowledge them. Call them by name. Breathe in their scent. Study their eyes. Examine their hair color, ears, neck, freckles, dimples, high cheek bones, eye color, and shoulder and body posture. Study them. Ask their likes. Dislikes. They're representatives of God's image, whether they know that Truth or not. Circle the relationship roles that God's given to you to nurture currently:

Sister	Grandmother	Sister-in-law
Wife	Friend	Daughter-in-law
Mother	Aunt	Girlfriend
Ex-wife	Mentor	Coach
Stepmom	Confidant	Image bearer of God
Caregiver	Neighbor	Employee
Business Owner	Colleague	Daughter
Adopted mom/child	Birth mom	Cousin
Boss	Acquaintance	Volunteer

Underline the relationships that you desire to improve. How can you apply "In everything, therefore, treat people the same way you want them to treat you..."?

♥ What relationships do you desire to work on first?

♥ Is there a toxic relationship that is sucking life out of you? What must you do?

♥ What healthy change are you willing to make that will enhance your relationships?

Enable Me, Lord, to Shift from not knowing how to treat people to treating people the same way I want them to treat me. Thank you, Lord. Amen.

Each life is an image bearer of God!

Enable Me, Lord, to Shift from believing I have no time—to *learning how to use the time God has allotted to me.*

DAY 2

So teach us to number our days that we may present to You a heart of wisdom. (Psalm 90:12 NASB)

We often say or hear, *I don't have time for that*, yet we plop on the couch, give our time to TV, video games, or turn our face to our cell phones to check the latest social media, game, or chat box. Do we deceive ourselves? Do we think we can find real life on social media? Yet we immerse ourselves in the virtual world, risk nothing, hide behind a screen, and disengage from real life. We become passive. Could this be an escape, to protect us from learning how to deal with real, live relationships? The Word says, "So teach us to number our days that we may present to You a heart of wisdom" (Psalm 90:12 NASB).

Time is God's gift to us. He gives us life and breath 24 hours in a day. Only God knows the number of our days here on earth. To have relationships requires an investment of one's time. Do we make time for real-life face-to-face conversations? Let's take stock:

♥ Do you want to grow in your relationships? Circle yes or no.
♥ Do you want to grow in your marriage relationship? Circle yes or no. Then you must spend time together. Conversation time. Shared experience time. Work time. Growing time. Love time. Play time.
♥ Do you want to grow in girlfriend relationships? Circle yes or no. If so, step out. Risk. Be the first to ask a friend to join you for coffee or a walk. Engage.
♥ Do you want to become a better parent or grandparent? Circle yes or no. Learn how to give your child or grandchild time. Discover who they are. What do they like to do? Where do they want to go? Make the time.

Let's dig down one more layer in our self-assessment about where we spend our time.

♥ Where do you spend most of your awake time? Why?

♥ Who do you spend your time with?

♥ Does your time distribution contribute to lasting Kingdom purposes?

♥ Is there something you spend time doing that you feel God wants you to give up?

For example, I recall the day I stood in the elementary school hallway. A 40 year-old mom of one of my students shared her story with me. It was then that I realized I wanted to invest more of my time listening, encouraging, and empowering women, instead of returning to the classroom and teach little loves to read. I needed to shift where I invested my time. I took the next step by faith and went to Life Purpose Coach ® training. "... Teach us to number our days that we may present to You a heart of wisdom" (Psalm 90:12 NASB). We have one life, that's it. No do-overs. We never get to erase a day. How we invest our time counts for eternity.

To drive home the message about the importance of time, go back to the beginning of this devotional and circle the word *time* every time it's used. Each time you draw a circle around the word *time*, visualize minute-by-minute, hour-by-hour, and day-by-day where you invest your *time* with someone, something, or on social media. How many *times* did you circle? ____ Did you like what you saw in your mind when you circled the word *time*? If not, shift and begin investing time in the relationships God has given to you!

♥ What do you need to stop doing that is robbing you of relationship time?

♥ What do you want to do instead?

♥ What will you do to take steps toward that goal in a relationship?

Enable Me, Lord, to Shift from believing I have no time, to understanding that there is a limited amount of time that God has given me to do everything He has for me to do. Give me wisdom to invest my time in the relationships You desire for me.

Teach me, LORD, how to use my limited resource of time for Your glory.

Enable Me, Lord, to Shift from a life of separation—
. . . to *reconciliation.*

DAY 3

Now all these things are from God, who reconciled us to Himself
through Christ and gave us the ministry of reconciliation,
(2 Corinthians 5:18 NASB)

Picture an upright vacuum cleaner standing in the corner of the living room. Normally, a round cylinder runs up and down inside the machine. It's empty, until we suck up dust, dirt, hair, or maybe our pet's fur. Sometimes the machine gets a clog from a hairball or two in the long suction hose. So we unlatch the canister, empty the cylinder, and poke something down the hose to dislodge the hair and dust balls. Then we plug the vacuum back in to check the suction and yea! The intended function is restored, and we continue sucking up grime and grit.

Picture ourselves like that vacuum cleaner, standing alone in our living room with a heart-shaped cylinder within us that runs the length of our core. We scoop up life stories that are filtered through our perceptions: rejection, self-loathing, guilt, regrets, and misunderstandings. The debris is messy. Our shame, lies, and self-talk clog us up. Yet, underneath the clog of our messy, broken stories, a relationship ache gnaws at us as if our soul has separated from our body. We're starved for connection. So how do we reconcile ourselves to our Creator's intended relational state so we can prosper in life doing what we were created to do?

Reconcile: It means to restore, align, tune, conform, harmonize or synchronize. Since we're created beings, we're meant to be restored and reconciled to the God-man who made us.

I pray that every person who reads this devotional will grasp this Truth to the core of their soul: "Therefore if anyone is in Christ, *he is* a new creature; the old things passed away; behold, new things have come. Now all *these* things are from God, who reconciled us to Himself through Christ and gave us the ministry of reconciliation, namely, that God was in Christ reconciling the world to Himself, not counting their trespasses against them, and He has committed to us the word of reconciliation. Therefore, we are ambassadors for Christ, as though God were making an appeal through us; we beg you on behalf of Christ, be reconciled to God. He made Him who knew no sin *to be* sin on our behalf, so that we might become the righteousness of God in Him" (2 Corinthians 5:17-21 NASB).

It's simple. Pull out your heart-shaped cylinder before God, confess the scum and sin from your life (anger, jealousy, addictions, remorse, dirt, broken relationships, pride, sinfulness and shame to name a few) and dump them at His feet. Then ask Him to be your Savior and restore your heart to Him as your Reconciler and Redeemer. "Who reconciled us to Himself through Christ and gave us the ministry of reconciliation." Now rejoice and ask Him to be your source of power through the Holy Spirit to do the work He has created for you to do.

♥ What do you need to empty out of your heart-shaped cylinder?

♥ When did or will you pray a reconciliation prayer to your Creator?

♥ Who can you tell that you have prayed to receive Christ?

Enable Me, Lord, to Shift from a life of ache, angst, and separation to a life of reconciliation with my Creator God. Amen.

Reconciliation = Reconciled

Enable Me, Lord, to Shift from believing
I am not known—
to *having confidence that I am known.*

DAY 4

O LORD, You have searched me and known me.
(Psalm 139:1 NASB)

We want to be known. Recognized. Discovered. Accepted. Believed-in. Acknowledged. Affirmed. Loved. Enjoyed. To *just be.* Comfortable in our own skin. Real. Closely connected to others.

Yet, a battle wages, a war *for* our hearts and in our hearts to destroy our personhood. The road to being known is strewn with land mines.

♥ Pride rears up and gets in the way. Sin blocks our path.
♥ Other peoples' sin is spewed on us, like poison that eats away our flesh and our health. Lies seep into our spirit, stealing our joy and eroding our freedom.
♥ Sin multiplies and seeps deeper. Lust. Greed. Addictions.
♥ We choose our masks—performance, beauty, wealth, prestige.
♥ Fear encapsulates our hearts, and we erect walls of self-protection.
♥ We position shields to avoid exposing our messy broken hearts.

Perfectionism. Workaholism. Control. Beauty. Busyness. People pleasing. Power. Position. Prestige. Money. Status. Knowledge. Circle your mask(s). Or write one in _____ .

Shields (circle yours). Alcohol, anger, greed, jealousy, substance abuse, secrets, abuse, TV, porn, withholding, negativity, or other addictions. We love them more than life itself. What do they require from us? Show up and submit. Our shields steal our life. They rob us. We know they're not healthy. But to trust Jesus, His Word? That's a risk and a leap.

31

Yet Jesus says, "He has searched me and known me." Drop the shield. Tear off the mask. Run to the Man of His Word. Scripture is clear. Psalm 139:1 states, "I have searched you and known you." Just as a flashlight shines light on our pathway, Jesus' caring eyes see into our inner being. He knows when we stand, where we sit, the number of hairs on our head, the tears we leak, or will leak, where we live, what we are up to, what is well and what is wrong. He knows it all.

Live with the Truth as your footing—*I am known*, no matter if anyone in my life gives me the time of day. Jesus knows me.

♥ God knows you. How does that resonate with you?

♥ Are you waiting on someone to know you? If so, can you release them from that expectation and believe that Jesus knows you?

♥ Name the shields that you are hiding behind. Will you throw them aside and receive the Truth? Jesus knows you.

Enable Me, Lord, to Shift from believing I am not known to having confidence that I am known. You are my God, a relational Father and my Creator. Thank You, Lord. Amen.

I am known.

Enable Me, Lord, to Shift from isolation—
… to *bearing one another's burdens.*

DAY 5

Bear one another's burdens, and thereby fulfill the law of Christ.
(Galatians 6:2 NASB)

Wounded by women in her past, Michelle was weary of offering her heart. But her fast-paced life as a full-time registered nurse, a wife, a mom, and grandmother, was driving her further from female touch points. Yet, she craved friendship! She needed HELP!

Webster's dictionary states, "Loneliness is cut off from others, not frequented by human beings, and produces a feeling of bleakness or desolation." Whew, not frequented by human beings, like a vacant soul. By her mid-forties Michelle was ready and willing to take a step. She walked into a mid-week ladies' class at her church. To her surprise a former high school friend attended. These two women celebrated the same birth dates, plus they birthed sons on the same dates, and they shared similar heartfelt needs. What timing, a God appointment! They had not seen each other for years. Feeling safe in the class and reconnecting with a friend Michelle slowly opened up and shared her heavy load of deep loneliness, bleakness, and desolation since she isolated.

After weekly times of sharing, connecting, and learning Michelle walked lighter and freer. She rejoiced that she stepped into a ladies class and bonded with more women than the former friend.

Scripture is clear, "Bear one another's burdens, and thereby fulfill the law of Christ." We were made to be in relationships. Make it a purpose to connect share, confess, be honest, rest and just be, all in authenticity. Look at Jesus as our model, the great God-man, He had 12 disciples and three best buds. So why shouldn't we connect? Do life with others and not isolate.

Today, Michelle's calendar is a bit full as she balances her roles, and one role is leading the women's ministry at her church. Just think, what if she had never taken the first step out from isolation to connect, care, share her burden, and hear from others in the class? She would have missed out on relationship joy!

♥ Do you isolate on purpose? Why? If so, what fear drives that?

♥ What step can you take toward a circle of community to confide and share your burden and listen to others burdens?

♥ Name someone you would like to connect with?

Enable Me, Lord, to Shift from isolation toward connection to others and pray for each other so our loads in life maybe lighter. Thank you, Lord. Amen.

Connect. Share burdens.

Enable Me, Lord, to Shift from my plan of
becoming a mom—to trusting that *God will instruct
and teach me in the way I should go.*

DAY 6

I will instruct you and teach you in the way which you should go;
I will counsel you with My eye upon you. (Psalm 32:8 NASB)

I rode an emotional monthly roller coaster of my cycle as questions tossed me about: *What if I never conceive? What if I do conceive? What if I miscarry?* Tests and tears became my companions. My longing for a baby lasted days, months, and years but my plan was continually thwarted. Infertility became my new buddy, definitely not my BFF. I desperately needed to make a mental shift.

I read this verse, "I will instruct you and teach you in the way which you should go; I will counsel you with My eye upon you" (Psalm 32:8 NASB). I prayed, waited, listened, sought counsel, as well as God's counsel. He led.

- I stepped through the doorways of several specialists' offices.
- I waited and prayed.
- Then I completed visits to an adoption agency.
- I waited and prayed.
- I traveled to two hospitals, three years apart, and paced anxiously while two determined birth mothers gave birth to my daughters. First, I became a mom to a beautiful redheaded daughter. Second, I became a mom to an adorable babe with curly brown hair.
- Ten years later I flew across the Atlantic Ocean and fitfully slept during a thirteen-hour train trip that took me deep into a former Soviet country. Finally, I set my eyes upon the green-eyed talented nine year-old boy who would be my final arrow. "I will instruct you and teach you in the way which you should go; I will counsel you with My eye *upon* you."

Each child had been a thought in God's mind. Each of their birth parents had carried the DNA mix to bring forth my two daughters and one son. Each of my children were created in the image of God and carried to term. They were released into my arms to love, care for, and nourish as their mom.

Adoption. Planned. Wanted. Treasures. These words are packed with significance for me. I am so thankful I never conceived and am a mom to my three children. I'll love them forever. God's watchful eye was present and directing their destiny and mine long before we were ever born. How can I help but love Him?

♥ What plan of yours isn't going as you hoped?

♥ If you haven't already, when will you pray this verse, "I will instruct you and teach you in the way which you should go?"

♥ What one step can you implement and "step into" accordance to His leading?

Enable Me, Lord, to Shift from my plan to trusting that You will instruct and teach me in the way which I should go; and You will counsel me with Your eye upon me. Thank You, Lord. Amen.

God leads. Watch for it.

Enable Me, Lord, to Shift from denial regarding
a relationship—to *knowing the truth,*
and the truth making me free.

DAY 7

So Jesus was saying to those Jews who had believed Him,
"If you continue in My word, then you are truly disciples of Mine;
and you will know the truth, and the truth will make you free."
(John 8:31-32 NASB)

I stood near my brother's casket and asked God if I were lying in the casket, *What would my life legacy be?* I shuddered. Authenticity is woven into my Terrell genes. Plus Jesus lives within me, and the words of Scripture pounded through my head: "You will know the truth, and the truth will make you free."

I couldn't die in a lie. My heart was broken, and my pent-up pain seeped out. I felt safe at the funeral home, near my roots, the farm, and surrounded by my family and friends—safe to ask God, *Where had Darlene Terrell disappeared to?*

Days after the funeral, on a hunt to figure out why I was still alive, I dug into a beaten-up cardboard-box that contained my college and high school yearbooks, trophies, and scrapbooks. I flipped through my yearbooks and read affirming comments from my high school teachers and friends referencing my leadership qualities.

Months later, a Life Purpose Coach® had mentioned my leadership strengths when she glanced over my summaries of my high school and college years. I frowned in response to her words. *Where had I gone?* What other said didn't match what the most influential man in my life at that time was saying about me. *Really?* The observations didn't match. What was going on? Who was I? Who did I believe? Who was telling the truth? And who was lying? I slowly found the answer, and the following definitions helped me.

Denial means to *not accept or believe the reality of a situation*. One day I found myself kneeling on our bathroom floor preparing to pierce my palm. This was the day I realized I was living in the center of a critical war of deception. My body, soul, and spirit were exhausted. I was ignored every time I spoke an opinion. I was blamed for all things. I was the object of emotional manipulation. I did not recognize that I was being abused.

If you have never lived with an abuser or known someone who has experienced abuse, you will have a hard time understanding and relating to the way an abused person is treated and how they feel.

A warning, when you hear the word abuse, be wise. True abuse is consistently enacted by one person or a group of people over a period of time. Merriam Webster's online Dictionary states **abuse** is: *a corrupt practice or custom, improper treatment, language that condemns or vilifies usually unjustly, physical maltreatment and or a deceitful act.* Abuse grows, and toxicity is the main ingredient in abuse. A toxic person is filled with poison and spreads that poison to others. Would you want poison poured on you?

The definition of Domestic Violence comes from the United Sates Department Office on Violence Against Women. Domestic violence is "as a pattern of abusive behavior in any relationship that is used by one partner to gain or maintain power and control over another intimate partner. Domestic violence can be physical, sexual, emotional, economic, or psychological actions or threats of actions that influence another person. This includes any behaviors that intimidate, manipulate, humiliate, isolate, frighten, terrorize, coerce, threaten, blame, hurt, injure, or wound someone." https://www.justice.gov/ovw/domestic-violence

Notice, the definition does not say domestic violence is only physical abuse. Domestic Violence is all about power and control. It is destructive.

"Emotional abuse is not normal. Emotional abuse is the consistent pattern of being treated unfairly and unjustly over a period of time, usually by the same person or people. It can also be a onetime traumatic event that is left unresolved. Emotional abuse is an intentional assault by one person on another to so distort the victim's view of self that the victim allows the abuser to control him or her" defined by author Dr. Gregory

38

L. Jantz, page 12. And "Emotional abuse keeps you from understanding and envisioning the person you were created to be." Page 17

When you live in domestic violence and emotional abuse for over 25 years, you're brainwashed to believe you have no worth. That's why during my abusive relationship, I tore-out and shredded the pages of positive comments from my high school yearbooks. But, "you will know the truth, and the truth will make you free" and once I understood the truth of my story, Truth, Himself, led me out of denial step by step.

♥ Are you stuck in denial in an area of your life? Name it. Who will you tell the truth to?

♥ Do these definitions resonate with you or make you think of a person? If so, please have them read this devotional. If this touches you, how so?

♥ If you are in an abusive relationship, who can you trust with your story?

♥ You will contact them by:

Enable Me, Lord, to Shift from denial regarding
a relationship to the Truth, You.
Thank You, Lord. Amen.

Jesus is Truth.

Jantz, Gregory L., and Ann McMurray. Healing the Scars of Emotional Abuse. Grand Rapids, MI: Revell, 2009, page 12 and from page 17 of his book.
If this devotional resonates with you, I highly recommend you read all of the *Enable Me, Lord, to Shift* devotionals to help with your healing journey and to grow.

You have read seven devotions.
I want to give you permission if you need more time and or want to
review a day or two or three, go for it. Stop right now and journal your
thoughts of what you want to refocus on for a day or two
or another week. Your growing is what is crucial,
not if you complete this book in 31 days.

Have fun. Stretch and grow and apply!

Enable Me, Lord, to Shift from believing I am abandoned—to believing *God is with me always to the end of the age.*

DAY 8

...and lo, I am with you always, even to the end of the age.
(Matthew 28:20b NASB)

I waited for the moving truck that carried my husband and three teens to disappear down the driveway. Then I dropped to the top step of the porch and sobbed. I was abandoned, alone, left behind.

Merriam Webster's online dictionary defines *abandoned as to withdraw protection, support, or help.* And indeed, my husband was pulling the plug on our marriage, which was actually reality catching up. Mentally, emotionally, and financially, he had abandoned and abused me for many years. Yet physically, this would be the first time in over twenty-five years I'd be on my own. Doubt hounded and haunted me. My fears multiplied. *How will I make it? Can I make it?*

Abandonment is on women's fear list. We worry and wonder and play the *if game. What if my status changes? How could I go from married to divorced? Married to widowed? How will I make it? Can I make it?* If a woman has been financially abused and/or a stay a home mom for years, fear hounds her to run. She wonders if her relationship status will cause God to change.

Oh, NO! God doesn't change or lie or move away. No matter our status; whether single, married, divorced, married to an abuser, and/or widowed, shift to embrace the Truth to what Jesus says, "I am with you always, even to the end of the age" (Matthew 28:20b NASB). Erase our false belief that we are on our own. Paste this verse into our heart and walk as if Jesus is holding our hand.

I stood up, wiped my runny nose and tears and opened the burgundy front door. Silence enveloped me. Memories consumed me. Emptiness lingered. That last night at the house on the hill and all the nights to come, Jesus was and continues to be my comfort and guide.

♥ Do you live with the fear of abandonment? How is that fear crippling your current relationships?

♥ Name a forward step you can take to put a stake in the ground so you will not allow this fear of abandonment rule your life.

♥ Memorize this verse and state it aloud, "And lo, I am with you always, even to the end of the age" whenever you sense the lie of abandonment creeping close.

Enable Me, Lord, to Shift from believing I am abandoned to knowing You are with me to the end of the age. Thank You, Lord. Amen.

God is with me to the end of the age.

Enable Me, Lord, to Shift from not asking God—
to *letting [myself] ask of God . . .*

DAY 9

*But if any of you lacks wisdom, let him ask of God, who gives to all
generously and without reproach, and it will be given to him.*
(James 1:5 NASB)

Dalice called from California. She was a thirty year-old single career woman. But her single life was far from ordinary. Three generations lived under her roof. I lovingly asked her questions so we could discover where she needed coaching.

The eldest person living in her home was her 89 year-old paternal grandfather. Next in the age lineup was her mother. She was in her mid-fifties, physically healthy, but recently widowed. Dalice's two teenage twin brothers lived with her too. Needless to say, emotions ricocheted from the walls of her house.

Dalice shed tears as she said, "The stress is too much. Grandpa is tugging on one ear, my siblings on the other ear, and my mom is in deep grief."

She needed wisdom. Stat!

We prayed, "But if any of you lacks wisdom, let him ask of God, who gives to all generously and without reproach, and it will be given to him" (James 1:5 NASB). After our prayer time, we talked about the specifics of her family dynamics.

- An elderly grandfather had to choose to grieve the loss of his son. Only he could mourn his loss.
- A wife lost her husband. Could Dalice do her mom's grieving? Absolutely not.
- Teenage sons saw their father die. Dalice hurt for her brothers, but she couldn't process her brother's grief on their behalf.

43

• And what about Dalice's loss? That was hers to own. Only she could grieve her loss.

•Considering the mix of ages, roles, genders, and personalities, Dalice was dealing with a dark kaleidoscope of reactions to death. Is there any wonder why she was stressed?

God offers us riches with this verse as He invites us "…Let him ask of God who gives to all generously and without reproach, and it will be given to him" (James 1:5 NASB). Are you lacking insight, discernment, or are you in need of clarity or direction? Do you share your questions with your Creator?

Dalice prayed for wisdom and gained understanding. She addressed urgent obstacles like family meal prep and her sibling's academic needs in high school. But she had to work through her own grief and honor her love for her father. Mourning is a recursive process that takes time.

Bring your questions to God and take part in discovering wisdom.

♥ Who do you usually take your questions to?

♥ How will you apply this verse in your life?

♥ In what areas of your life will you implement this verse?

Enable Me, Lord, to Shift from not asking, to asking You, God. I ask for wisdom, believing You will show up, and show me the way. Thank You, Lord. Amen.

God is the wisdom giver for all our needs.

Enable Me, Lord, to Shift from what others
have told me—to *believing, just as He said.*

DAY 10

He is not here, for He has risen, just as He said.
(Matthew 28:6a NASB)

Just as He said: only four words, but life changing.
Just as He said.
Who? Jesus.
What? Spoke.

In Matthew 28 Mary Madgalene and the other Mary come to look at Jesus' grave. The angel greets them and tells them, *"He is not here, for He has risen, **just as He said.**"*

Think about the power in those words! Jesus does what he says. What He spoke, He meant. What He promises is a promise. The entire Word of God hinges on the words *just as He said.*

To grow in wholeness in our relationships, it's crucial to know and trust those four words: *just as He said.* We plod through life's trials and tribulations. But we must first know what the man of Truth says instead of looking for what dad, mom, siblings, spouse, girlfriend, boss, church leader, neighbor or Facebook says. After all, God formed us and stamped His purpose upon our lives. Only God knows where our shoes will trend.

"...The LORD will provide..." (Genesis 22:14b NASB). *Just as He said*, Faithful Provider.

"...I am with you always..." (Matthew 20:28b NASB). *Just as He said*, Constant Companion.

"I have loved you with an everlasting love; therefore I have drawn you with lovingkindness" (Jeremiah 31:3b NASB). *Just as He said*, I love you forever.

"...God of all comfort. Who comforts us in all of our affliction..."
(II Corinthians 1:3b, 4a NASB). *Just as He said*, He comforts. Watch for it.

45

"I will instruct you and teach you in the way which you should go;" (Psalm 32:8a NASB). *Just as He said*, He'll instruct. Be ready. As God directs you and according to your need, seek counsel from the wise.

"THE LORD IS MY HELPER..." (Hebrews 13:6b NASB). *Just as He said*, He will help.

"A God who sees" (Genesis 16:13b NASB). *Just as He said*, He sees you now.

"A very present help in trouble" (Psalm 46:1b NASB). *Just as He said,* Call out to Him, be watching.

"I, the LORD, do not change" (Malachi 3:6a NASB). *Just as He said*, Rock solid Holy man.

"... And His name will be called Wonderful Counselor, Mighty God, Eternal Father, Prince of Peace" (Isaiah 9:6b NASB). *Just as He said*, All-sufficient God.

"God hath not given us the spirit of fear, but of power, and of love, and of a sound mind" (2 Timothy 1:7 KJV). *Just as He said*, Be fearless because you have God's power, love, and mind.

"...For You created all things, and because of Your will they existed, and were created" (Revelation 4:11b NASB). Just as He said, you were born for a divine destiny. He signed your life purpose ID.

The two Marys left the site of the tomb in awe and wonder and hightailed it to the disciples to give them the breaking news: up from the grave He arose, just as He said.

Run to the heart of God, the man of Truth. Saturate your mind in the Word. Believe every word you read. Jesus means what He says. Receive the Word. Digest it. Live it. *Just as He said,* the Word brings true comfort, reassurance, and hope.

♥ Name one of the verses (from above) that is suited to a need in your life.

♥ Write out how you will accomplish what this verse asks of you.

♥ What would you like to see as your outward growth with that verse?

Enable Me, Lord, to Shift from what others have told me to believing just as He said.

Just as He said.

Enable Me, Lord, to Shift from anger—
to *You, to help me master my anger.*

DAY 11

...sin is crouching at the door; and its desire is for you,
but you must master it. (Genesis 4:7b NASB)

Only Sara and Joe were on the clock, working in close quarters in a small coffee kiosk that didn't allow anyone in a corner of the bookstore to miss a thing.

Sara greeted guests, wrote the code for their drink on the coffee cup, and passed it down the counter. Then she deposited customer's cash in the register drawer as the customer line grew.

The hot drink barista, Joe, whipped up latte, mocha, or chai. He muttered under his breath, tossed the blender in the sink, and barked out names to customers. I cringed as I watched his frustration escalate from a nearby table in the bookstore. He steamed one latte after another, which seemed to match his mood. Underneath his breath he muttered angrily.

Sara offered a hand and was curtly told, "Stay at the register or the coffee corner."

I sighed as I prayed for these young adults. Joe repeatedly refused help from Sara. It appeared to be a form of self-torture related to a source of hurt or anger. Whatever it was, Joe was taking it out in the form of horrible customer service and a public temper tantrum. "Sin is crouching at the door; and its desire is for you, but you must master it."

Sara called her supervisor to send help. It was obvious Joe needed a break or was going to blow up. She came and washed dishes, took out the garbage, and got milk. As she continued to help, Joe exited a few steps out the front, bent over, then returned to the hot bar like a fighter entering the ring as he simmered in anger. He continued to prepare hot beverages while muttering angrily. Over the next two hours, his attitude escalated.

I sipped my mocha, wrote, watched, and listened, Joe's sighing and sulking drove Sara's anxiety up and placed her on eggshells. "...sin is crouching at the door; and its desire is for you, but you must master it." By now, anger had devoured Joe. I knew this war well. I'd battled with anger for years before I allowed God to diffuse it. It had furrowed deeper and deeper into my soul with each new hurt.

As believers, we have access to the power of the Holy Spirit if we ask for help. Unfortunately, Joe was trying to gut it out by sheer will. Anger "had" him. I prayed harder for him as I watched his rage escalate. He was about to come uncorked. Eventually, he left the kiosk again and then stepped back in the ring to fight it out. By now the anger monster had consumed three hours of his day. He looked tired, spent, and cornered. "Sin is crouching at the door; and its desire is for you, but you must master it."

Anger destroys lives and relationships. If Joe would have been a coachable client, and a female, I would have asked.

♥ Why are you so angry?

♥ Instead of reacting angrily, what do you want to say?

♥ What is your first step to cutting the power cord to anger?

Enable Me, Lord, to Shift from anger to You, to help me master anger. Thank You, Lord. Amen.

Grow up and out of childish ways.

Enable Me, Lord, to Shift from the death of my
dream—to *I fear no evil, for You are with me;*

DAY 12

Even though I walk through the valley of the shadow of death,
I fear no evil, for You are with me; (Psalm 23:4 NASB)

The house on the hill stood empty. I had one more job to finish to put closure on this chapter of my life. I carried the five snowman-shaped patio bricks to the tall oak tree west of the house. I dropped them in the dirt under the May sunshine and wiped my tears and runny nose. Only God was invited to this private memorial.

I dug five little graves side by side like cemetery plots. Then I placed each snowman face-up. Each was about a foot tall and dressed in winter garb with buttons for eyes, tube socks for hats, and torn sock fabric for the scarf frill. When they were young, each of my children had decorated his or her own snowman. Now I laid them all to rest in tiny graves.

The five snowmen had stood on the front deck steps and greeted guests as they entered the front door. Come on in and visit. They were heavy and had been nearly too much to carry as I walked through the valley of the shadow of death to take them to their graves. I'd decided they needed to be buried on the land where my husband and I had lived with our children and hoped to build dreams. Five graves represented the five lives that walked this property and lived as a family for 27 years, now finished. It was time to say goodbye and trust God to carry me through the next chapter of my life. Death had come to my dream. "Even though I walk through the valley of the shadow of death, I fear no evil, for You are with me;" (Psalm 23:4 NASB).

I covered the snowmen with dirt and prayed. Then I lifted my hands in surrender to God as I wept.

You gave me one husband and three children. I did my best to love, Lord, yet it wasn't enough. I was alone. Yet God was with me, invisible, but present. I stood, brushed the dirt from my knees and slowly walked to my red van.

Once I pulled out of the drive I could never return. *I fear no evil, for You are with me.* I turned toward my car and stepped toward a new life in faith.

♥ When have you *walked through the valley of the shadow of death* and/or the death of a dream?

♥ Where did you see God's hand in it?

♥ How was He with you?

Enable Me, Lord to Shift from the death of my dream to
I fear no evil, for You are with me;
Thank You, Lord, for Your faithfulness. Amen.

God is always with His children.

Enable Me, Lord, to Shift from avoiding pain—
to *feeling it and sowing in tears.*

DAY 13

Those who sow in tears shall reap with joyful shouting.
(Psalm 126:5 NASB)

The mother was young and pregnant with their first child. The baby was born dead, a horrific shock to the parents. They left the hospital with empty arms, tears, and demolished dreams. They opened the door of their home, only to close the baby's bedroom door, a room chuck full of pink frills and bibs, bonnets, bedding, and books galore.

Her husband handed her divorce papers. She recoiled and taped newspapers on her basement windows, changed the locks on her doors, and turned from the warning words of her pastor. She stopped counseling and blocked loved ones calls from her cell. She allowed one friend into her private pain. However, that person brought the wrong antidote, a nightly bottle of wine.

Abused as a child, she spun through her adult years in a frenzy of control: work, home, family, forcing her way. She told her husband what to do and when to do it. She blamed, cast doubt, second-guessed his actions all day long and whipped off one swear word after another to keep herself in a position of power. Trust a man, again? How could she? She'd trusted her father and he used her body for his pleasure. Avoid the pain, run away, and take control.

I grieve for these precious women. When I lost my youngest brother to a heart attack, I told God I *was pressing into the death pain.* I was worm out from the chaos of abuse, pain, the grief of my father's death, and my mom's failing health. I desperately wanted to live with joy. It's crucial we feel our losses and pain as we go *through* the valley. In time, joy sprouts.

Jesus is our model. "He was despised and forsaken of men, A man of sorrows and acquainted with grief; And like one from whom men hide their face He was despised, and we did not esteem Him. Surely our griefs He Himself bore, And our sorrows He carried; Yet we ourselves esteemed Him stricken, Smitten of God, and afflicted. But He was pierced through for our transgressions, He was crushed for our iniquities; the chastening for our well-being fell upon Him, and by His scourging we are healed" (Isaiah 53:3-5, NASB). Jesus felt pain. He was afflicted, pierced, smitten, spat upon, crucified. Jesus felt every tear in his flesh. Why? To show us His love for us and the way through pain.

Don't run from your pain-filled feelings; pool them in your heart and feel their pain-filled purpose. What do you want those feelings to tell you? Name it. Then hold that pain-filled hand up and open it to God. Pour out your pain. Weep and wrestle at the feet of the loving God-man. He'll meet you with open arms. He sees and hears. Ask Him to heal. Ask Him for joy. "Those who sow in tears shall reap with joyful shouting" (Psalm 126:5 NASB). Just you wait.

♥ What pain are you avoiding?

♥ What is your first step in acknowledging the pain?

♥ When will you tell a friend about your loss?

Enable Me, Lord, to Shift from avoiding pain to feeling it. And even if I have to sit for a while, help me begin to process my pain. Thank You, Lord. I want joy. Amen.

Joy comes.

Enable Me, Lord, to Shift from rejection—
to *loving one another.*

DAY 14

*Beloved, let us love one another, for love is from God;
and everyone who loves is born of God and knows God.*
(1 John 4:7 NASB)

Lee could barely breathe. She felt like her heart was being ripped from her chest. Her only child, Jimmy, a junior in high school, had asked to live with his father. The idea of separation from her son tore at her heart. To make matters even worse, Jimmy's father had spoke negatively to him about his mom and created hatred and a wall of separation between Jimmy and his mom. The rejection had decimated Lee! What father would do such an evil act?

Tia walked into her living room and immediately noticed the 8x10 picture of her and her husband facedown on the coffee table. Her heart froze with grief. Over the following days, her husband continued to leave rejecting messages for her. Even before the divorce papers arrived, his cowardly avoidance, silences, walkouts, and love for sin clearly demonstrated his rejection.

Mollie's daughter Chelsea was acting strangely. She was a new mom but overly protective of her one year-old daughter, Mollie's first grandchild. Mollie traveled to Florida to spend time with her daughter, but Chelsea didn't allow Mollie to hold her granddaughter or watch her alone. Yet, the other grandmother frequently visited, picked up and cuddled the baby, and was even allowed to baby sit. Mollie's heart ached with grief. What rejection! Why was her daughter withholding her grandchild from being loved by her own grandmother?

My heart hurt for each of these women. Rejection delivers a sharp, deep, crushing blow to the heart. The depth of the pain is multiplied when betrayal comes from a trusted loved one: son, husband, and/or daughter. What do you choose to do? Grow bitter or get better?

I recommend you run to God and His Word. He knows the Truth behind every situation and the depth of your pain. It's your choice grow bitter or to grow better by learning how to love, even when you face rejection:

1. Pour out your pain and rejection to God.
2. Invite the Lord and His lavish love into the raw, open wound.
3. Ask for His enabling to fulfill God's command to "love one another."
4. Receive His love as ointment.
5. Reject the rejection as final. Too many women fear repeated rejection, so they vow, never again. They place their heart in a lock-box, and self-sabotage the possibility of ever loving well. Don't allow others' selfish, sin-filled choices to limit your love life.
6. Focus on the God of Truth, and seek Him and His ways.
7. Imitate His love.
8. Keep asking for His refilling love. He is the source of love.
9. Again, reject rejection.
10. Only a pure, Holy, Intimate Father God who knows us inside and out can meet our greatest love void.

If you, my friend, have tasted rejection, what are you waiting for? Open up your heart to Him. Receive His love and "love one another, for love is from God; and everyone who loves is born of God and knows God." Continue to grow in love and give His love gift away.

♥ Do you live your life emotionally dependent upon your ex-husband, son, daughter, husband, mom, birth mom, father, birth father, or another person who rejected you?

♥ How long will you allow them to control your life? Release that need for control. Ask God for His restoring love.

♥ Who do you want to learn to love well with God's enabling?

Enable Me, Lord, to Shift from rejection to loving others, for love is from God; and everyone who loves is born of God and knows God. Help me love, Lord. Amen.

Love well, with God's unfailing love

You have read fourteen devotions.
If you need more time and or want to review a day or two or three, go for it. Stop and think about what you want to refocus on for a day or two or a week as you journal your thoughts. The most crucial thing is your spiritual growth, not whether you completed this book in 31 days.

Have fun. Stretch and grow and apply!

Enable Me, Lord, to Shift from denial—
to *desiring truth in the innermost being.*

DAY 15

Behold, You desire truth in the innermost being,
And in the hidden part You will make me know wisdom.
(Psalm 51:6 NASB)

It was garbage can day at my church. Not the day that the garbage was picked up; instead, it was the day our pastor challenged us to write out what was holding us back from knowing God. Quickly, I wrote down, all of me. Then I stood up, walked to the garbage can, pitched in the paper, and returned to my seat. I bowed for prayer.

Weeks prior to garbage can day I sensed God was up to something. I was a divorced woman, but I felt uncomfortable as men began appearing in my pathway. Then one man showed up closer. And of all places, in church. God got my attention.

I dove into the Word. For three months I studied scriptures that pertained to divorce and remarriage. I prayed and met with my pastor to review what God was teaching me through His Word, the Holy Spirit, and my story. My pastor listened and reaffirmed my understanding of the verses. Scripture spoke to me. To become a wise person—Truth must be known, then sown in the innermost being.

During my study time I discovered a pocket of denial in my heart. Denial is simply not admitting the truth. I was denying and ignoring my buried desire to be married to a God-fearing man. An inner duel between denial and desire created tension and duplicity and made me feel uncomfortable with men.

I voiced my desire and deleted my denial as God's Truth worked in my heart. According to God's Word, I was released to remarry a godly Christian man. Wisdom was sown. "…And in the hidden part You will make me know wisdom" Psalm 51:6 (NASB).

Do you want to be wise? Open up your Bible. Read. Invite the living Word of Truth into every corner of your heart so wisdom can grow. "Behold, You desire truth in the innermost being, And in the hidden part You will make me know wisdom" Psalms 51:6 (NASB). Give God all of you and your heart.

♥ What is holding you back from knowing God?

♥ What Truth do you need to sow into the hidden part?

♥ What wisdom did you learn from that Truth?

Enable Me, Lord, to Shift from denial and allow you to open up every area of my heart where I am holding back. You desire Truth and wisdom sown into our hearts. Amen.

Invite Truth into the inner being.

Enable Me, Lord, to Shift from not forgiving—
to *forgiving others, just as God in Christ
also has forgiven me.*

DAY 16

*Be kind to one another, tender-hearted, forgiving each other,
just as God in Christ also has forgiven you.* (Ephesians 4:32 NASB)

Mia shared with me about her husband of 25 years. After he passed away, she discovered his secrets: photos of him, his adulteress, and their private life. She'd had hunches.

Sallie spoke of an incident in her twenties. A businessman expressed interest in her startup business. He worked with her, encouraged her, only to turn on her and rape her.

Marla whispered through tears how her dad had snuck into her bedroom when she was about five years old. He sexually abused her then said, "No one will believe you if you tell." Her mom was often away for work and never found out.

Courtney told me her husband was ordered to pay spousal and child support. He moved from state to state in an effort to evade the law. Even Friend of the Court had difficulty squeezing funds from him.

Pain, heartaches, abuse, and betrayal slaughter the heart. Do we forgive or not?

I teach women to turn to the Word. The Truth says, "Be kind to one another, tender-hearted, forgiving each other, just as God in Christ also has forgiven you" (Ephesians 4:32 NASB). When we repeat the instruction backwards, we're told *Just as God in Christ also has forgiven you,* forgive *each other.* Jesus is our model of how to forgive.

Over ten years ago in my first counseling session, I was warned, "Darlene, if you get bitter, God will put you on a shelf." I decided right then that I wouldn't get bitter. I refused to waste the years of emotional pain I endured while my heart was mutilated by abuse. However, since that day in counseling, my betrayal has increased. Dr. Ramon Presson states in the Divorce Care workbook, "Forgiveness is like a book you need to check out again and again."

So how many times do we have to forgive?

According to the Word," Then Peter came and said to Him, "Lord, how often shall my brother sin against me and I forgive him? Up to seven times?" Jesus said to him, "I do not say to you, up to seven times, but up to seventy times seven" (Matthew 18:21-22 NASB). Forgive how many times? _____ x _____ = _____

So what does forgiveness look like? Let's learn from the opposite word: unforgiveness. If we choose not to forgive, our choice shuts us off from others. Unforgiveness stunts our spiritual growth. Weeds grow and stifle life from growing in us. Picture a garden hose. When it is twisted or kinked, water stops flowing. The same is true if we choose not to forgive. Unforgiveness chokes the flow of love from God-through-us-to-others. Spiritual nutrition and life become obstructed. It's impossible to receive God's love; therefore, we become desolate. Bitterness festers and we die. Jesus says to forgive. Who better to heed? After all, what did He say on the cross to His betrayers? But Jesus was saying, "Father, forgive them; for they do not know what they are doing" (Luke 23:34a NASB).

Ask for His help to forgive, just like Mia, Sallie, Marla, Courtney, and I did. When you ask for God's power to forgive, His love is unleashed through you, since He is the source of love. Only God's love enables forgiveness.

F – Father, help me forgive
O – Others and myself as the
R – Right next best step.
G – *God's grace forgives me of my sin. Thank you, Jesus!*
I – I choose to obey and forgive.
V – Victory is mine through Christ
E – Everlasting love from God enables us to forgive.

Release offense(s). Choose to forgive. Fill us with Your love, Lord. We then pass along Your love to others.

♥ Is there someone you need to forgive? Name them or give them a secret name.

♥ If you are refusing to obey God's Word and hurt yourself, explain why you make this choice.

♥ What can you do to symbolize an act of forgiving him/her or them?

Enable Me, Lord, to Shift from not forgiving to trusting You, Father, to help me forgive others and myself as the right next best step. God's grace forgives me of my sin. Thank You, Jesus! I choose to obey and forgive. Victory through Christ and everlasting love from God enables us to forgive. Thank You, Lord. Amen.

Obey. Forgive. Love.

Enable Me, Lord, to Shift from not voicing—
to *declaring Your mighty acts.*

DAY 17

One generation shall praise your works to another,
and shall declare Your mighty acts. (Psalm 145:4 NASB)

My sixteen year-old son Elliott and I traveled to my sister's for Thanksgiving. Having him with me was a gift, as he lived with his father. As I drove down the highway, I pulled out a list of questions that were geared for around-the-Thanksgiving-table conversation. I asked, "Can you see anything God aligned in your life over the last year?"

"I can't see a thing," he said.

I cringed. Sadness and remorse threatened to swallow me. I feared that my son would turn away from God. I shared how God had provided my car, clients, training and more over the last year. Scripture states, "One generation shall praise your works to another, and shall declare Your mighty acts."

After our Thanksgiving meal my sister asked Elliott if he would like to do a few jobs. He hauled her Christmas tree upstairs, unwound the lights, and strung them on her tree. Then he set up a lighted tree outside for her. When he finished, she presented him with a surprise —a brand new waffle maker. Elliott was speechless.

Unbeknownst to my sister, the previous night Elliott had studied the Black Friday ads. He told me he would like a waffle maker. Elliott had spent his formative years in an orphanage, and because the food of his childhood was simple, a waffle maker was a special gift. Twenty-four hours after he voiced his wish, God had provided Elliott with his desire.

When we headed home later that evening, I said, "We need to revisit the question I asked this morning, "Where have you seen God align things in your life?" We reviewed the day's surprises, and the waffle maker was at the top of Elliott's list. "One generation shall praise your works to another, and shall declare Your mighty acts."

We never know how much time we have to speak Truth to a loved one. Guard the time. Invest it. Speak Truth. Elliott returned to his father's the next day.

♥ When do you want to take advantage of a time to share His Word with the next generation?

♥ Who do you want to speak to about the Truth?

♥ What is burning on your heart to share with your children, grandchildren, or other young people you love? Pray and prepare words to share.

Enable Me, Lord, to Shift from not voicing to being bold to declare Your mighty acts with the next generation. Thank You, Lord. Amen.

Share and show off God's goodness.

Enable Me, Lord, to Shift from believing no man stands by his word—to *believing according to all that He promised; not one word has failed of all His good promise.*

DAY 18

Blessed be the LORD, who has given rest to His people Israel, according to all that He promised; not one word has failed of all His good promise, which He promised through Moses His servant.
(1 Kings 8:56 NASB)

L et's read that verse slowly, "Blessed be the LORD, who has given rest to His people Israel, according to all that He promised; not one word has failed of all His good promise, which He promised through Moses His servant." "Not one word has failed of all HIS good promises." Astounding—banking our life on God and His Word promises alone solid-rock stability.

However, for women who have experienced the heart-wrenching pain of sexual, mental, physical, and/or emotional abuse; divorce, rape, betrayal and any form of deception from a male, this Truth is tough to accept and take to heart. Jesus is a man of His Word. He walks His talk. Yet trusting is a wrestling match for many women because empty words fell to the ground for soul-deadening years and even decades.
Examples from women's lives:

• He said he loved me, my daddy that is, but he sexually abused me.

• He said he cared about me, but he never asked about the details of my life, didn't respect my opinions, and ignored my presence.

• He texted me often and said we would meet, yet he never followed through.

• He said he would marry me, but he never did. He only used me for sex.

67

• He said he would take me out on a date, yet he used the time to attack my character.

• He said he would stop smoking pot, but instead he hid it in his dresser.

• He said he didn't need to converse with me, his wife, yet he talked freely with another woman.

• He said he would help with the housework, but he sat in a chair and played video games.

• He vowed until death do us part, but he walked out of a counselor's office and filed for divorce.

Many women's relationships with men have been marked by empty promises, vanity, narcissism, unfaithfulness, and arrogance. Yet, let me clarify that there are good honest men who speak the truth and carry it out. My father was such a man. He made a vow to my mom, and they stayed together almost 52 years before my father's unexpected death. He wasn't perfect and hurt my mom at times, and I saw gaps in their communication. But women and men must learn that only one person is sufficient to fulfill all our needs, and that is Jesus Christ.

Let us choose to be intentional about believing Truth. Jesus is a man of His Word. He is the Truth Man. The Truth God-Man. The Lord promised Israel He would lead them. The Lord promised Israel He would provide for them. The Lord promised Israel freedom from oppression. The Lord promised them a Messiah. Jesus was born. We could go on and on with examples of promises fulfilled. "Blessed be the LORD, who has given rest to His people Israel, according to all that He promised; not one word has failed of all His good promise..." We must drive this Truth home to our hearts. God is a man of His Word. What He says He will do, He will do!

♥ What domain (spiritual, mental, emotional, relational, financial, physical or life purpose) in your life do you doubt God's Word?

♥ Why do you believe you doubt in this area?

♥ What verse can you sow into your heart to receive the Truth and put the doubt to death?

Enable Me, Lord, to Shift from not believing You are a man of Your word to the Truth that You are a man of your Word. What You say You will do. Who You are is who You are. Thank You, Lord. Amen.

God is a vow keeper!

Enable Me, Lord, to Shift from not confronting—
to *speaking the truth in love, we are to grow up in
all aspects into Him who is the head, even Christ.*

DAY 19

*We are no longer to be children, tossed here and there by waves and
carried about by every wind of doctrine, by the trickery of men, by
craftiness in deceitful scheming; but speaking the truth in love, we are to
grow up in all aspects into Him who is the head, even Christ,*
(Ephesians 4:14-15 NASB)

When I was nine years old and in fourth grade, and our class was a bit boisterous that day. Mr. V., my teacher said, "The next student who talks without raising his or her hand will have to eat soap." Without thinking, I shouted out my answer. He came to my desk and cut off a piece of soap for me to eat. Tears of humiliation flowed like a faucet from my eyes and dripped from my nose. That day in school, I learned that it's better to keep my mouth shut. And since I disliked confrontation, why not?

Scriptures says, "We are no longer to be children, tossed here and there by waves and carried about by every wind of doctrine, by the trickery of men, by craftiness in deceitful scheming; but speaking the truth in love, we are to grow up in all aspects into Him who is the head, *even* Christ" (Ephesians 4:14-15 NASB). By my early 40s it was necessary for me to learn to practice this verse.

Stuck dead center in a cobweb of fear from living in an environment of domestic violence, I had to learn to stand up and grow a backbone. I asked questions to try to gain clarity about our life so I could understand what was happening and stop worrying. But my abuser threw accusations, doubt, blame, venomous words, lies, and arguments back at me. Of course, I wasn't without fault. I attacked verbally and was critical until God got control of my tongue. Once He convicted me of the hurt I was causing, I learned to regulate my words. I needed to learn to speak out without reacting. I often got "stuck" in a reactive mode and didn't know how to speak truthfully with love. But God had a plan to teach me how: exchange students.

I introduced our exchange students, teenage girls, to each room in the home including the bathrooms. I clearly explained to them to use a small amount of toilet paper, not a handful. I also told them to "Wrap up used feminine products and put them in the wastebasket. Then take the garbage out to the trash before garbage pickup."

On a Sunday afternoon I was in desperate need for a nap when I heard, "Mom, the toilet is overflowing." I'd already been practicing speaking truth with love, so I offered up a bullet prayer before I went to explore. My children were laughing at their father, who was using the plunger on the overflowing toilet. This was not the first time this mess had occurred. My unspoken words boiled. I wanted to take our female exchange students aside and give them a tongue-lashing. I knew my words were too HOT to address right then. Instead, I grabbed old towels to sop up the urine-covered floor and give myself time to let the anger die down. Then I took the plunger and finally got the "issue" to go down. I fumed. I prayed. What was I going to do?

I would sabotage the message I wanted to communicate if I spoke loudly. *God, help me,* I prayed. I finally met with the girls and reviewed what I'd asked of them. They listened. BUT, I made certain they heard and understood the consequences.

"If this happens again, whoever comes out of the bathroom last will be the one who will clean the floor and wash all of the towels. Do you understand what I'm saying?"

I was growing up spiritually. "We are no longer to be children, tossed here and there by waves and carried about by every wind of doctrine, by the trickery of men, by craftiness in deceitful scheming; but speaking the truth in love, we are to grow up in all aspects into Him who is the head, even Christ." I walked away from that confrontation singing inside. I spoke the truth in love.

♥ What is most challenging for you regarding confrontation?

♥ How can you use bullet prayers during confrontation?

♥ Who do you need to speak to with truth and love?

Enable Me, Lord, to Shift from not confronting to speaking the truth in love; we are to grow up in all aspects into Him who is the head, even Christ. Help me practice this Truth, Lord, thank You. Amen.

Speak the truth in love.

Enable Me, Lord, to Shift from believing I am of no value—to *I am valuable.*

DAY 20

Are not two sparrows sold for a cent? And yet not one of them will fall to the ground apart from your Father. But the very hairs of your head are all numbered. So do not fear; you are more valuable than many sparrows. (Matthew 10:29-31 NASB)

One day at my apartment complex, I went outside to walk and worry. I looked up and there at the end of the roof perched a little bird, high and lifted up for the whole world to see. As I looked at it, it chirped. In time it would fly, swoop over ponds, eat bugs and worms, sing its lovely song, plus leave droppings. As I watched the bird, I thought of this verse, "Are not two sparrows sold for a cent? And yet not one of them will fall to the ground apart from your Father..."

If that obscure bird took a nosedive off the ledge of my two-story apartment building, God would see it. He has a watchful eye. The rest of the verse says, "...But the very hairs of your head are all numbered. So don't fear; you're more valuable than many sparrows."

We are loved, loved, loved. Valued, valued, valued. You ask, *How so? Loved? Valued? Bring it on, because I don't believe that.*

Again, the Truth says, "Are not two sparrows sold for a cent? And yet not one of them will fall to the ground apart from your Father. But the very hairs of your head are all numbered. So do not fear; you are more valuable than many sparrows." The Word doesn't say God counts the bird's feathers. But the verse does say He counts His created image bearers' hair, (yet) He also knows when a bird falls. God is that personal and intimate. He hones in on our body and life details.

When my daughter asked me to attend her ultrasound appointment, I saw God's handiwork up-close. Since I never carried a child, the experience was new, and I was thrilled to be asked. I gasped in awe to see a baby created in the image of God right there on a monitor screen. I asked the ultrasound tech, "What's the area near her head that looks like sparklers?" She answered, "It's her hair."

My granddaughter's hair was lighting up. I came home and looked up this verse. I wrote my granddaughter's name, Anastasia, in my Bible. *God knows the very hairs of your head. And He commands us not to fear, as we are of more value than many sparrows.*

To think God's watchful eye knows all. For goodness sake I am created in His image, have a soul, and He knows my hair count? How much He loves you and me and tells us not to fear!

God's got me. He's got you. He desires us to trust Him with His enormous love and believe in our value. Put a stop to the "not good enough" "what if" and "worry wort" mind traps.

♥ What part of this verse do you believe and what part don't you believe?

♥ What can you do to sow more of this verse into your heart?

♥ How can you practice this Truth?

Enable Me, Lord, to Shift from believing I have no value to believing I'm more valuable than a sparrow. Yet, You know when one sparrow falls, so how much more is Your love for me, when You know the number of hairs I have. May that cause me not to fear.

God knows the number of hairs I have.

Enable Me, Lord, to Shift from single life—
to *relationships.*

DAY 21

*God sets the lonely in families, he leads out the prisoners with singing;
but the rebellious live in a sun-scorched land.* (Psalm 68:6 NIV)

The day is a sunny Sunday afternoon in July. The place is a yellow ranch-style home tucked into a wooded subdivision. The backyard is shaped like a half circle. Trees fence in the property. The grandchildren arrive, and 11 year-old Henry, 9 year-old Samantha, and 6 year-old Molly explore their private playground.

Love is on display—simple life, simple care, food, love, kindness, and kickball to boot.

Family togetherness.

Harmony.

Peace.

Love.

Joy.

Serenity.

My new husband's laughter is joy-filled and deep.

His daughter Jaycee asks, "Is it okay if I do a load of laundry?"

Brutus, the grandchildren's large chocolate lab, sprawls on the lush green grass.

My husband's response to Brutus leaving his droppings in the yard? "Jordon...?"

"Yes, I'll get a shovel."

I drink in words of acknowledgement, respect, kindness, and care. The atmosphere breeds safety and security to be one's self.

Papa Sam, Henry, Samantha, and Molly ride bikes down Hathaway Drive. Papa Sam is engaged and participating. These everyday experiences are precious and simple.

My husband's youngest son Jack sits and plays games on his cellphone, yet pauses thoughtfully to help me with my printer.

Jordon kicks back, long-legged in a gravity chair, snoozing as his children play in the garage.

Henry asks, "Can I use chalk on the garage floor?"

The Larson Lunch counter opens. I serve brownies and ice cream while Molly, Samantha, and Henry dream about what life will be like at an older age. They offer me their stories, their minds, their hearts as they pretend and have simple fun as children.

These experiences are new for me. Thrilled, I savor safety in a home with children and grandchildren. Peace hovers over the house, a true gift of family. Children are allowed to be children. Laughter, bikes, football and kickball mark the time. Adults are valued for being themselves. No one attacks the heart: *You should, You'd better, or You need to.* Instead— Grace. Love. Safety. Protection.

Thank you, Lord! You give back as promised. "God sets the lonely in families, he leads out the prisoners with singing; but the rebellious live in a sun-scorched land" (Psalm 68:6 NIV).

Jaycee prepares to leave. I hug her and without hesitation and say, "Jaycee, we love you." Young Molly steps into the van, then turns to me and says, "I would like you to come to my house and see where I live."

Invited.

Precious.

♥ Who has God brought to be your family?

♥ What people do you miss?

♥ Where can you go to expand your relationship circles?

Enable Me, Lord, to Shift from a single life to see where You want me involved in relationships. Thank You, Lord. Amen.

God is for relationships.

You have read twenty-one devotions.
If you need more time and or want to review a day or two or three, go for it. Stop right now and journal your thoughts about what you want to refocus on for a day or two or another week. Your spiritual growth is crucial, not if you completed this book in 31 days.

Have fun. Stretch and grow and apply what you're learning!

Enable Me, Lord, to Shift from grief—
to *choosing to rejoice and be glad in it.*

DAY 22

This is the day which the LORD has made;
Let us rejoice and be glad in it. (Psalm 118:24 NASB)

I thank God for two women. Both cheered me on as Hearts with a Purpose Advisory Board members and dear friends. Please rejoice with me when you read my books, as they are answers to these women's prayers.

Connie and Phyllis were single women who met in their early fifties at a Bible Study Fellowship leaders' meeting. They loved studying and teaching God's Word to women. Connie was a high school physical education teacher, and Phyllis an office administrator at a large trucking company. Each had a dream to own a house on a lake. So their friends encouraged them to buy a house together. They listened to their friends and asked them to pray with them for one year about the house decision. And so they all prayed.

After a year, the two friends sensed a green light from God. Then a realtor friend called to tell them a house on a lake was available. However, it was located further north than what they were looking for. They decided to check it out anyway.

Connie and Phyllis walked through the main level of the home. Then Con went upstairs to check the layout. She quickly called Phyllis to come up. In the upstairs hallway Connie looked out the west window and her eyes took in a beautiful lake. When she turned to look out an east window, she gasped: a second lake.

They prayed with their realtor, then put down a bid. The realtor said, "I've never prayed with clients before." She suggested they raise their bid, as she knew a higher offer was on the table. The two friends said, "No, our price was what we felt led to offer. If God wants us to have the house we'll get it."

Later that day their phone rang. Their realtor congratulated them. The homeowner wanted Phyllis and Connie to be the new owners of the house that sat on not one lake, but two. How big our God is! Con and Phyllis' new life sharing a house together on the two lakes began.

For years the two friends enjoyed woodcarving, Bible classes, camping, fishing, and trips to Florida when Michigan's temperatures dropped. Time flew by quickly.

When they reached their seventies, their health began to wane. First, Connie was diagnosed with Parkinson's and Myasthenia Gravis. Phyllis willingly became her caretaker, believing it was a part of her life purpose. However, Phyllis was diagnosed with cancer in the midst of her caretaking years. The disease took her life at the age of 77. Con deeply grieved her friend's passing. They had shared over 24 years together. Trips, Bible studies, fishing, family, camping, meals, holidays, and living in the same home together. They had shared a rare gift of friendship.

When I coached Connie, she was grieving the loss of her health and Phyllis's death. One thing Phyllis had said every morning to Connie, *"This is the day that the Lord has made, I choose to rejoice and be glad in it"*. Connie too wanted to learn to be positive but needed time to process her grief.

1.   She wrote Phyllis a good-bye letter and read it to me. This helped give her closure, since her failing health had kept her from being at Phyllis' bedside and at her memorial.

2.   Connie viewed Phyllis' memorial service on her iPad.

3.   Connie wrote about and read to me the things she missed most about Phyllis.

4.   She discovered some of Phyllis's notes about her role as Connie's caregiver. It comforted Connie's heart to read Phyllis's personal thoughts.

5.   Connie worked on giving thanks to God for her friend when memories overwhelmed her with sadness.

6.   Con read often from the book of Psalms.

And as Connie progressed, she said, "I must stay positive as Phyllis would tell me, *"This is the day which the LORD has made; I choose to rejoice and be glad in it."*

♥ Are you facing grief? If so, write about it.

♥ What steps can you implement to help you process the loss?

♥ Can you memorize this verse and choose to rejoice in the day?

Enable Me, Lord, to Shift from grief to rejoicing in all You have given to me. Help me grieve and process. But also shift my thoughts to, this is the day that the Lord has made, I choose to rejoice and be glad in it.

Choose to rejoice, today!

Enable Me, Lord, to Shift from empty emotional eating and drinking— to *hungering and thirsting for righteousness in relationships.*

DAY 23

Blessed are those who hunger and thirst for righteousness, for they shall be satisfied. (Matthew 5:6 NASB)

Leslie's kitchen was her domain. She prepared scrumptious meals that ranged from salmon, turkey, steaks, chicken, beef, or wild game grilled, roasted, fried or baked to your desires. Her skills in cooking and baking whetted everyone's taste buds. Food was her passion and her pride…and her indulgence.

Her doctor had warned her, "You are diabetic. Change your eating habits and exercise." She needed to drop 60 pounds. Yet every night after the kids went to bed, she devoured a bag of potato chips. Her husband longed to have her come to bed, read a book, be close by, make love, and simply be near him. Instead, Leslie chose her comfort: food.

Leslie reached out to me on Facebook. "Write about emotional eating." I am not a dietician, therapist, or doctor, but I was led to this verse, "Blessed are those who hunger and thirst for righteousness, for they shall be satisfied." I suggest you pray this verse if righteousness is not your heart's desire. God is the master of heart changes.

The Truth says, *those who hunger and thirst for righteousness* shall be blessed and satisfied. We all long for satisfaction. But we must slow down and take inventory of our mind and body's reactions and responses.

Listen. Learn. Quiet your mind and body long enough to explore what you're really longing for. Investigate. Ask. What is it I want? Am I really hungry? What emotion is stirring inside me before I shove something in my mouth? Will this glass of beer, cookies, or chocolate solve any ache I have? Why do I run to this instead of the Truth? "Blessed are those who hunger and thirst for righteousness, for they shall be satisfied."

We are all a bit like Leslie. Only she knows why she didn't move toward her husband. But could it be because she had put on weight? Was she fearful of rejection, so she stayed away from her man? Yet her emotional eating sabotaged her relationship. Move toward healthiness in relationships. God desires a wholeness that only He can bring. After all, righteousness means doing right.

♥ Instead of food, beer, chocolate, what do you truly want?

♥ Relationally, what do you long for?

♥ When can you start praying this verse aloud?

Enable Me, Lord, to Shift from emotional eating, drinking or _____ to hungering and thirsting for righteousness. Thank You, Lord. Amen.

Righteousness satisfies.

Enable Me, Lord, to Shift from my weakness—
to *relying upon the Spirit Himself who intercedes.*

DAY 24

In the same way the Spirit also helps our weakness; for we do not know how to pray as we should, but the Spirit Himself intercedes for us with groanings too deep for words; (Romans 8:26 NASB)

My body revolted. It was as if he placed his deer rifle to my stomach and pulled the trigger. BOOM! My intestines twisted and wrenched as I thrashed. Gut-wrenching groans rose from my throat as I crumpled to the floor to pray.

Never had I battled such an internal war. Morning, noon, and into the evening, I collapsed with groans on the living room rug or bedroom floor. On my knees, head bowed, prayers, tears, hatred, and cursing spewed from me.

Forgive me, Lord. I don't know how to do this. I don't even know how to pray right now.

I wanted to hate. I felt as if I was at war. Yet God reminded me of this verse: "The Spirit also helps our weakness; for we do not know how to pray as we should, but the Spirit Himself intercedes for us with groanings too deep for words;"

Help me, Lord, I whispered. I wiped my tears, stood, and went on to face one more day.

My hunter husband heard and saw nothing of my agony. He had packed up his guns, head mounts, and headed to his hideout when he set in motion his sin-motivated step to divorce me. He made sure the divorce papers were delivered through registered mail.

Why did he file, you may wonder? Me too. His excuses were lame, including the last: "You may never understand why I am doing this." BOOM!

87

"The Spirit also helps our weakness; for we do not know how to pray as we should, but the Spirit Himself intercedes for us with groanings too deep for words;" God hears, always. He's near and available—always. God responds to His children's cries, always.

I prayed aloud in our silent home. I knew the Truth—God was with me. He was present, even though it felt like my words ricocheted from wall to wall. I pushed toward God and voiced my pain aloud to struggle through my pain with Him. I flung acrid, bitter words, like a dagger, to stab my hunter husband's heart—not God's.

I mustn't give up on God. He's all I have.

I listened for directions from God. *Get better not bitter, Darlene. Don't waste your life on him but empty yours for Me.* "The Spirit also helps our weakness; for we do not know how to pray as we should, but the Spirit Himself intercedes for us with groanings too deep for words;"

The months passed in a haze of tears, as well as texts, prayers, visits, and support from family and friends. Praise was sacrifice. Walking with women friends was soothing balm. Tears still flowed, but I found the strength to move forward in small steps.

I pushed-in close to God. Closer and closer.

"Stay beside me, daughter. No space allowed. You can't risk that. Your heart is raw. You loved well, with your heart wide open. Push forward, but surrender to the depth of your pain—to the death of trusting that he was a man of his word, who would honor vows. It costs to love, my daughter. I know. I'll help you heal. Lay him down. Let him go. Trust me."

To win is to love. To forgive is to love. Love is my choice. Love always wins.

♥ When have you been weak?

♥ Did you turn to God in prayer and, if so, how did you sense the Spirit interceding for you?

♥ What good has come from your groaning?

Enable Me, Lord, to Shift to You when I am weak so the Spirit Himself can intercede for us with groanings too deep for words.
Thank You, Lord.

God intercedes in our weakness. Will you let Him?

Enable Me, Lord, to Shift from giving up on God and
church—to *not forsaking assembling together...
but encouraging one another...*

DAY 25

*not forsaking our own assembling together,
as is the habit of some, but encouraging one another;
and all the more as you see the day drawing near.*
(Hebrews 10:25 NASB)

Deb learned of the horrific news of her husband Jim's diagnosis
of cancer on a sunny spring day that marked their 21st wedding
anniversary. Life was in full throttle for Jim and Deb, who were raising
three high school daughters and a college-age son. With Jim's diagnosis,
stress, sickness, and sadness steamrolled into their family. How could it
not? Jim was only 42 years old as he began the fight for his life.

Our church body rallied to send meals, watch, wait, weep, and pray
for God to heal Jim. Yet God had a different plan. Our hearts leapt to Deb.
How should we encourage her?

We four friends, Deb, Debra, Susan and I, had met at church. Deb
and Debra scrapbooked together for years, and Susan and I met at a Bible
study. We four knew each other, as our children were similar ages and
were involved in birthday parties, church programs, and youth group
together. But Deb's pain-filled loss as a sister-in-Christ drew us together
as a ring of friends. We joined hands, carved time out, and dedicated a
night together every few weeks, to check in and a checkup: "How you
doing, Deb?"

We met for a meal at a home or a restaurant. We listened. Laughed.
Loved. Wept. And we shared prayer needs. If we didn't see one another
at church, we asked and pursued. "Not forsaking our own assembling
together, as is the habit of some, but encouraging *one another*; and all

the more as you see the day drawing near." We wanted to be His heart, hands, and feet to keep Deb close and connected to the church body, as her days were full, fast paced, and pain filled.

Since then, years have passed. All four of Deb's children are married, and she's celebrating being a grandmother. Susan moved, due to her husband's job change. Our ring of friends continues, as these women have embraced me through the upheaval of my life: from abuse, through divorce, to singlehood. And then a new marriage for me, where we all celebrated new love and suddenly the shock and devastation of an abrupt divorce. Then a major move for me from my church family of 34 years, where we had all met.

But, Deb, Debra and I still meet every 6-8 weeks for a meal. Before we hug each other goodbye, we select the next date and who will pick the next restaurant. Social media and texting allows us to stay in touch between meeting times.

So what if? What if we wouldn't have attended church? What if we wouldn't have reached out and joined a ring of friends? I can't imagine the precious loss of friendships. Don't miss out. "Not forsaking our own assembling together, as is the habit of some, but encouraging *one another;* and all the more as you see the day drawing near...as is the habit of some, but *encouraging one another..."* Connect, care, and look at the women who attend your church through God's eyes. Ask God for insight. He'll lead you.

♥ Is there someone you've been wanting to encourage at your church?

♥ You will reach out to them by _____.

♥ If you've stopped attending church, when will you go back? How can your attitude influence the experience positively?

Enable Me, Lord, to Shift from giving up on God to going to church and encouraging someone and keeping on encouraging.
Thank You, Lord. Amen.

Everyone needs encouragement.

Enable Me, Lord, to Shift from my relationship with
Social Media—to *a closer relationship with You...
a God, who sees.*

DAY 26

*Then she called the name of the LORD who spoke to her,
"You are a God who sees"; for she said, "Have I even remained
alive here after seeing Him?"* (Genesis 16:13 NASB)

Dear woman who is starving to be seen and heard, I write this from a heart that cares for you. My passion is to care for, connect with, and coach women to become fully alive to all God has created them for. Please read this love letter devotional to the end with those thoughts at the forefront of your mind. *I care about and want God's best for you.*

God has much more for you than Facebook, Instagram, Snap Chat, or text relationships can offer you. I know you desire meaningful relationships, but social media cannot provide true, meaningful relationships. I'm an author, and I understand the role of technology and social media in today's world. But as a Life Purpose Coach®, I am intimately aware of the dangers. As I share examples from women's stories, ask yourself, "Does this story parallel my experience? Is God speaking to me?" If so, I want you to know that you have the power to choose to change with the Lord's enabling.

✓ What is the motive behind posting silly, ridiculous, and meaningless details about when you got up, how you slept, when you ate breakfast and what you ate and who you ate with? Posting insignificant details about your life communicates a cry for attention and casts you in a negative light.

✓ Facebook is your life diary. When you post personal details and opinions, you ask for people's affirmation of your actions and words

95

through their responses or lack of response. You are, for all practical purposes, seeking a significance rating. Why is it important to do this with people you are not engaging with in real space and time? Wouldn't you prefer investing in a real, face-to-face relationship?

√ You're at work and on the clock, but you pick up your phone, shoot off a group message that makes fun of someone you work with, and then quickly put your phone back on your desk. Or you sneak time to text a friend and play video games.

What? How would your employer respond? Are you being paid to be on your phone? Are you stealing time from your employer? Regularly? Do you feel comfortable about it?

√ You're out to dinner with friends, but you can't take your eyes off your text messages and email. Have your virtual relationships grown more important to you than the people sitting next to you? Is a name on a screen more important than the living, breathing person beside you?

√ *He texted me you say* with glee. Yet, he never shows up and you never lay eyes on him.

Relationships over a cellphone or group chat are simply communication over a device. Social media can be a great tool, a way of connecting and communicating in a large community. I use it daily, but it doesn't provide eye-to-eye, hand-to-hand, doing-life relationships, and this is what we crave.

I ask, dear friend, have you bowed in prayer and asked your Creator to guide your communication before you clicked on Facebook, Snapchat, or Instagram? God wants you to know Him and spend time with Him, and He wants to be the Lord of all your life. In Genesis 16:13b, Hagar, a used and abused maid of Sarai, runs away to the wilderness to escape her mistress' harsh treatment. Hagar had no social media and was totally alone–or so she thought; but God was with her. He saw Hagar and heard her. Hagar was astounded and said, "You are a God who sees..."

Look up this passage of scripture, Genesis 16:13. God sees you at home, in your dorm, at your apartment or condo. He sees you at work, at war, weeping, or at worship. He sees you.

Ask the Lord to enable you to shift from your relationship with social media to a more intimate relationship with the God who sees you. He's that personal. He hears your cry and has His eyes on your every need. What a God He is!

♥ What is it you want God to see about you?

♥ What is it you want God to help you with?

♥ How much time will you step away from social media and give to God? On what date will you start this commitment?

Enable me, Lord, to Shift from Facebook and social media posts to spending more time with You and knowing You are a God Who sees me. Amen.

God sees you!

Enable Me, Lord, to Shift from not listening—
to *listening and hearing.*

DAY 27

A wise man will hear and increase in learning...
(Proverbs 1:5a, NASB)

Years ago my words were falling on deaf ears. Accusations toward me were common. I decided to evaluate the accusations to see if there was any truth in them, so I stopped talking and tuned into my self-talk. I also listened to my accusers words as objectively as possible.

I pictured his words landing in a sieve above my head. I asked God to sift out my accuser's truthful words. The words that remained in the sieve would be truth I needed to work on. But if blame and lies leaked through the sieve of truth, I would let those words go. They were meant only to hurt, bully, intimidate, and threaten me into submission. And yes, I discovered areas I needed to grow up and out of, and always his words were wrapped in fear.

I kept listening and using the sieve of truth. As time passed, my hearing grew more discerning, and my listening led me through the process. This scenario makes me think of the story of Bartimaeus, who was short one sense, yet his listening skill helped him compensate.

In the book of Mark, chapter ten in the Bible we read of Bartimaeus. He was a blind beggar. He sat along the road one day when Jesus was coming through his town. "When he heard that it was Jesus the Nazarene, he began to cry out and say, "Jesus, Son of David, have mercy on me!" Many sternly told him to be quiet, but he kept crying out all the more, "Son of David, have mercy on me!" (Verses 47 and 48). Jesus responded. Thankfully, Bartimaeus persisted calling out and did not listen to the naysayers. Instead, he relied upon his hearing. If he hadn't, he may have missed his divine appointment. His sight was restored that day!

According to the Word of God, "A wise man will hear and increase in learning..." (Proverbs 1:5a, NASB). The word hear is a synonym for listen, according to Merriam Webster's online dictionary, and it states, listen means the following:

1. To give ear to,
2. To pay attention to sound,
3. To hear something with thoughtful attention,
4. To give consideration,
5. And to be alert to catch an expected sound.

Let us pick this definition apart. Give ear to; well that means I am willing, I am open. And to pay attention to a sound is like heading to the door when the doorbell rings. Don't you take action or respond? If you heard a child cry, would you not investigate? If you are paying attention, you are ready to do something, like putting away your cell phone, closing your laptop, shutting the TV off, or stopping the game before the digital world swallows your communication skills.

To hear something with thoughtful attention is to hear behind the words of what the person says. Consider. Learn. Don't think you know it all. Ask questions. Never assume. Hear and learn what is not said. Glean. Expect the unexpected sound. I think of a man, I will call him, Joel. I loved watching him at church. Whenever he saw his wife, he stopped and tilted his head down to her level. Then he cocked his ear to catch every word from her lips. His interactions made me smile. He loved his wife, so he tuned into her. I knew he was a wise man.

♥ Where do you need to grow in actively listening?

♥ What is the first step you need to apply?

♥ In what other area of your listening skills do you want to grow?

*Enable Me, Lord, to Shift from not listening to actively
listening and hearing. Thank You, amen.*

A wise woman hears.

Enable Me, Lord, to Shift in grief—
to know, I have prayed for you,
that your faith may not fail...

DAY 28

But I have prayed for you, that your faith may not fail; and you, when
once you have turned again, strengthen your brothers.
(Luke 22:32 NASB)

Longtime friend, mentor, Bible study partner and colleague Pat walked into my living room. She sat down on my red couch and said, "Darlene, I am praying that your faith will not fail you." Then she opened up her Bible and read this verse aloud, "But I have prayed for you, that your faith may not fail; and you, when once you have turned again, strengthen your brothers" (Luke 22:32 NASB).

Two and a half years into our marriage, my husband pulled the trigger and filed for divorce. His sin-filled action swept my feet out from under me and sorrow pulled me under. His actions made a mockery of a vow and made me want to vomit. I clung to the fact that God existed. He was alive and present with me. But I desperately pleaded with God for answers to what had happened to our marriage.

My husband and I had met at a church where I'd attended for over 30 years. He initiated introductions and asked me my status. I said, "Divorced." He said, "God hates divorce but not those that are divorced" and told me that he was a leader in a divorce recovery group. We talked off and on that year. Two years later he asked me out, pursued, courted, and proposed to me, even down on one knee, and of all places, at church. He wanted a church wedding, and we picked out a home together with all the furnishings. It looked like God was turning my life around and giving me a God-fearing husband, a mid-life marriage, a family, and a home filled with His love.

During his abandonment, I went outside one spring day to walk. My eyes caught a red flicker. Hovering above the large landscape rock across the street were not one, two, or three cardinals, but four. I had been told that cardinals show up when grief arrives. They were like kisses from the King as a reminder that God was with me and aware of my pain, since I often asked Him, Why?

Months later, I went to seek counsel from a counselor friend about Hearts with a Purpose. Stunned, Jan referenced the same verse as Pat, "I have prayed for you, that your faith may not fail; and you, when once you have turned again, strengthen your brothers." Jesus spoke these words to Peter in the book of Luke after Satan sifted Peter. I rested in knowing, "Jesus was praying for me that my faith may not fail." The verse was a reminder to me that my husband's abandonment and cruelty didn't diminish who God was.

The best medicine a woman can use when she experiences grief is the Word of God. Believe. Receive. "And you, when once you have turned again, strengthen your brothers." That is what I am doing at Hearts with a Purpose: coaching, speaking, teaching, and writing on behalf of hurting women to strengthen them in the Truth.

♥ Do you sense your faith is failing? If so, name who you can tell.

♥ What is the best way for you to process your grief?

♥ Name one thing you can do to stay in the Word.

Enable Me, Lord, to Shift in grief to knowing, Jesus has prayed for me... that my faith may not fail...thank You, Lord. Amen

Jesus prays for you.

Enable Me, Lord, to Shift from comparison, envy, gossip, greed, and jealousy—to *clothing myself with humility toward others.*

DAY 29

...and all of you, clothe yourselves with humility toward one another, for GOD IS OPPOSED TO THE PROUD, BUT GIVES GRACE TO THE HUMBLE.
(I Peter 5:5b NASB)

Five pride-packed words destroy relationships. For this devotional, think of them as five friends. They feed off each other as users and takers: Ms. Comparison, Ms. Envy, Ms. Gossip, Ms. Greed, and Ms. Jealousy.

To have healthy relationships, Ms. Humility must be included in all relationships "...and all of you, clothe yourselves with humility toward one another, for GOD IS OPPOSED TO THE PROUD, BUT GIVES GRACE TO THE HUMBLE" (I Peter 5:5b NASB). So how do we clothe ourselves with Ms. Humility?

Ms. Humility sees people as equal, created in the image of God with a soul. She recognizes her friends' need for a Savior since her messy life was broken and sin filled at one time. Yet Jesus forgave her, set her free from self-righteousness, perfectionism, and calling her own shots in life. Because of His grace, God's riches at Christ's expense, Ms. Humility desires that her loved ones also come to know Christ's transformational redemptive work. *Befriend her, clothe yourselves with humility.*

Now for the five friends we want to unfriend. Ms. Comparison starts the sin ball rolling. A woman sees Janelle has long shiny hair, and Judy has short white two inch stubs that stick straight up. We raise one up and put the other down. Human opinion becomes our ruler or standard of measurement to live by. Yet the Word says, "... but they measuring themselves by themselves, and comparing themselves among themselves, are not wise" (2 Corinthians 10:12b KJV). To become wise, unfriend

105

comparison. Instead, *clothe yourselves with humility toward one another.* Janelle wears her hair this way and Judy wears hers that way. Neither is better or worse, right nor wrong because hairstyle is purely a matter of preference.

Ms. Envy wants what someone else has. Leah has a new sparkly diamond. Janey must have that too. She sets her eyes upon what someone else has to make her arrive to their status. Scripture says, " envying, drunkenness, carousing, and things like these, of which I forewarn you, just as I have forewarned you, that those who practice such things will not inherit the kingdom of God" (Galatians 5:21 NASB). Envy leads to things and more things and eventually pure emptiness. Unfriend envy; instead, *clothe yourselves with humility toward one another.* Humility says, "I am happy for her. Leah can afford a sparkly new diamond. The truth: I cannot."

Ms. Gossip communicates negative and questionable information to other people that does not pertain to them. Michelle tells Irene about her neighbor Ellen's affair. Irene shares the news about Ellen with *her* neighbor. But why? What is their purpose for sharing hurtful information? To hurt someone.

A gossiper is also called an idle mouth, tattletale, or busybody. The Word warns, "At the same time they also learn *to be* idle, as they go around from house to house; and not merely idle, but also gossips and busybodies, talking about things not proper *to mention*" (1 Timothy 5:13 NASB). Unfriend gossip. Instead, *clothe yourselves with humility toward one another.* Humility speaks words of kindness and truth. Michelle talks directly to her neighbor about the damage to a family if she is having an affair.

Ms. Greed has an intense selfish desire for things such as food, wealth, sex, money or possessions. Greed grasps. Greed obsesses. Greed idolizes. Becky has a history as a stripper. She views porn, and then acts out the lust greed by having sex. The Word warns, "And they, having become callous, have given themselves over to sensuality for the practice of every kind of impurity with greediness" (Ephesians 4:19 NASB). Unfriend greed, instead *clothe yourselves with humility toward one another.* Humility is being content with what I have, *thank you, Lord.* And Becky learns the preciousness of her body and says, "NO" to lust greed.

Ms. Jealousy fears someone is going to take what she has. Jeany loves her 22 year-old son yet despises her son's new wife. Jeany doesn't want to share the only man in her life. "For where jealousy and selfish ambition exist, there is disorder and every evil thing" (James 3;16 NASB). Unfriend jealousy; instead *clothe yourselves with humility toward one another.* Humility recognizes that everything we have and everyone we know is on loan to us from God. Jeany learns this truth by recognizing she does not own her son and embraces her daughter-in-law.

Let's make certain when we send out relationship invitations that we "...Clothe ourselves with humility toward one another, for GOD IS OPPOSED TO THE PROUD, BUT GIVES GRACE TO THE HUMBLE." (I Peter 5:5b NASB).

♥ Which of the five pride-packed friends is wrecking your relationships?

♥ What do you need to do to grow in humility?

♥ Who can you tell for accountability purposes that you will unfriend the five?

Enable Me, Lord, to Shift from comparison, envy, gossip, greed, and jealousy to clothing myself with humility toward others.

Dress with humility.

I cover each of these sin filled friends in separate devotionals in *Enable Me, Lord, to Shift*, books #1 #2 and #3.

Enable Me, Lord, to Shift from me—
to *You to bear more fruit.*

DAY 30

Every branch in Me that does not bear fruit, He takes away; and every branch that bears fruit, He prunes it so that it may bear more fruit.
(John 15:2 NASB)

It was April, a spring Saturday in MI. I sat on our back deck drinking in the spring sights and watching my four year-old granddaughter play kickball. Suddenly, I heard an odd noise like someone sharpening knives and the click of metal upon metal. I glanced to my right; no movement in the woods. Then looked to my left to our closest neighbors, and no sound stirred from their yard. My eyes darted straight ahead into thickets and woods. I saw movement. It was my neighbor, Jim. What is he doing?

I studied his steps as he walked across their yard. From one tree to another, bent over, with pruning clippers, he snipped.

Aha! That was the metal noise—BIG scissors being used. My body bonded to the noise. My heart felt sliced and clipped.

It had been over a month since I'd received divorce papers. People sometimes symbolized death by a divorce contract for a second marriage, which for me was the lowest rung on the ladder of life. I'd never wanted one divorce, but a second? It represented everything I detested: irresponsibility, ignoring God's Word, and throwing our vows to the curb. Just the thought of the word made me sick and sad.

And the SHAME. No one could understand my shame. I could envision Satan drooling, "Let's bury Darlene."

"Why God, why?" The divorce did not make sense. The questions rolled through my mind. I knew I was to have a front row seat for my

109

neighbor's pruning lesson. The timing was too ironic. What did God want to cut out of me? Pruning does cut out and cut back, for better growth and to bear more fruit.

"What do you want from me, God?" I voiced my question, and then I spoke aloud what I knew to be true of God:

1. He intimately knew me and what was happening to me.
2. Like seeing through glass, He was aware of every matter of my heart.
3. He was aware of what I was reading that spring and summer, a book on the Lord's Prayer and praying "not my will, but yours, God." Now I found myself at an intersection.
4. My will? I wanted to remain married. But, if my husband chose to exit, I could not control him.
5. So what was God cutting away? A husband, a home, family life, pride, self-righteousness, and self-sufficiency.
6. What else? I often refer to a quote from Tony Evans: "God either causes things or allows things." And in this manner, He allowed a second divorce.
7. But what about my will? Yes, that was it, my will.

Snip. Clip. Exchange it—mine for His.
Embrace God and *Enable Me, Lord, to Shift* from me to You.

♥ When have you been pruned, or are you being pruned right now?

♥ What growth occurred or is occurring?

♥ What fruit do you still desire?

Enable Me, Lord, to Shift from me to You to bear more fruit.
Not my will, but Yours. Thank You, Lord. Amen.

Not my will, but God's, to bear more fruit

Enable Me, Lord, to Shift from doing relationships my way—to *fearing God and keeping His commandments, because this applies to every person.*

DAY 31

The conclusion, when all has been heard, is: fear God and keep His commandments, because this applies to every person.
(Ecclesiastes 12:13 NASB)

This verse leaves no wiggle room. It's a point-blank command. The author of Ecclesiastes, Solomon, is summing up his pursuit of his life purpose, as he tried it all: learning, sex, money, pleasure—all was vanity. "The conclusion, when all has been heard, is:

♥ fear God

♥ keep His commandments

♥ this applies to every person

Yet, aren't we like Solomon? We seek advice from parents, spouses, siblings, friends, pastors, doctors, professors, philosophers, authors, musicians, teachers, technicians, children, astrologers, Facebook, Snapchat, magicians, and or horoscopes to name a few of our sources. And for what purpose? To gain knowledge, sift through information, pick and choose what we like best. To be our own god.

Yet what about God?

"Who?" you may ask.

God.

He is the Creator: of you, every human being, and me. Open up the Word, Genesis 1:1,

"In the beginning..." then down in verses 27-28, "God created man in His own image, in the image of God He created him; male and female He created them. God blessed them; and God said to them, 'Be fruitful and multiply, and fill the earth, and subdue it; and rule over the fish of the sea and over the birds of the sky and over every living thing that moves on the earth.'" And then over in Genesis 2:21-24, "So the LORD God caused a deep sleep to fall upon the man, and he slept; then He took one of his ribs and closed up the flesh at that place. The LORD God fashioned into a woman the rib which He had taken from the man, and brought her to the man. The man said, 'This is now bone of my bones, And flesh of my flesh; She shall be called Woman, Because she was taken out of Man.' For this reason a man shall leave his father and his mother, and be joined to his wife; and they shall become one flesh. And the man and his wife were both naked and were not ashamed."

Run to the Creator of our souls for His advice on relationships. Men. Women. His idea. Marriage—His idea—His plan, between a man and a woman. Friendships. His idea, read of David and Jonathan, Ruth and Naomi, Mary and Elizabeth, Mordecai and Esther, for example.

Make a sticky note to self: God is three in one, relationally being, Father God, Jesus the Son, Holy Spirit. We are relational beings; our Creator God knows what ingredients are needed in relationships. Let's seek His advice first.

Next, we're to *Fear God*. Fear God? What is that? Reverence Him. Worship. Honor Him. Respect. Don't take His name in vain, like *"Oh G _ _."* He's the Alpha and the Omega. The designer of our body. The lover of our souls. The Savior of our life. The magnificent counselor, God of all comfort. Bow down to Him. Give Him your life, surrender to all He has for you. Hold Him in a rightful position in your heart, mind, and life. It's a choice to fear God through obedience in a relationship, rather than to try to get what you want. Two words, *Fear God* and *keep His commandments.*

Keep His commandments? Yes. We are asked to obey commandments like Love the Lord thy God, love your neighbor as yourself, encourage one another, be kind, tenderhearted, speak well, forgive one another, fear God, and many more wonderful commandments. And some of God's *don'ts* are for our good: don't steal, don't commit murder, don't covet, don't be jealous, don't commit adultery, don't divorce your spouse just because, don't get drunk, don't gossip, don't fear, don't be greedy, don't lust and many more. These are to protect us within and for relationships. *Keep His commandments.*

This applies to every person. You. Me. Look to your left, look to your right, the person you live with, who sits next to you, and the person you work with. "The conclusion, when all has been heard, is: fear God and keep His commandments, because this applies to every person" (Ecclesiastes 12:13 NASB). What more is there to say? How will you sow this verse into your relationships?

♥ Where in your life do you need to fear God?

♥ What sin do you need to starve out of your life?

♥ Where in your relationships do you need to obey a commandment?

Enable Me, Lord, to Shift from doing relationships my way to fearing God and keeping His commandments, because this applies to every person and that includes me. Amen.

Fear God and walk out His Word.

115

WRAP UP TIME!

Congratulations, you have completed the relational domain book of the *Enable Me, Lord, to Shift* series. My hope and desire is that you have made inroads to create healthier relationships by allowing the Truth to control more of your responses instead of reactions.

In closing, I would like you to take a pen or pencil and flip back to the BIG Assessment on page 11 that you shaded in over 31 days ago. Now, I would like you to draw a cross in the little heart in the center of the page. That little cross represents what Christ did for you and me. Because of His death on the cross we have freedom for the asking, if we apply the Truth to our life with the empowering and filling of the Holy Spirit since we are in relationship with Christ. He will enable you to spread Truth into each domain of your life setting you free to live.

Look at your BIG Assessment on page 11 and see which domains you need help in next. Is it the mental, spiritual, or emotional domain? I suggest you read each devotional book to help you grow in that domain.

Once you have read and applied the Word to your life, watch how freedom from the Truth will spread into each domain of your life. You then can take your pencil or pen and go back to your Big Assessment on page 11. Now draw the little cross lines longer and wider as your relationship with God spills and spreads over into every other domain, bringing God's Word alive in all areas of your life. God's way works, offering you freedom to live!

Also, do not forget to go back and check over your relational domain report card.

A closing comment, I love to stay in touch with my readers and be in community.

Please email me at Darlene@Heartswithapurpose.com and tell me how the book changed your life. Also, join Hearts with a Purpose readers and sign up to receive the weekly complimentary coaching newsletter, free to you, at www.Heartswithapurpose.com. And if you are in need of a coach or women's speaker for your event, contact me. I love to coach, speak, teach, and write on behalf of the needs of women.

God Bless you, Coach Darlene Larson

The first four books in print are:

Enable Me, Lord, to Shift: Are you stuck in idle? Learn how to shift into Truth and live!
Book 1, Spiritual Domain

Enable Me, Lord, to Shift: Are you stuck in idle? Learn how to shift into Truth and live!
Book 2, Mental Domain

Enable Me, Lord, to Shift: Are you stuck in idle? Learn how to shift into Truth and live!
Book 3, Emotional Domain

Enable Me, Lord, to Shift: Are you stuck in idle? Learn how to shift into Truth and live!
Book 4, Relational Domain

The physical, vocational life purpose, and financial devotionals for the *Enable Me, Lord, to Shift* series will be in print in late 2020 and 2021. Keep checking www.Heartswithapurpose.com for updates. Each book is a product of Hearts with a Purpose. www.Heartswithapurpose.com

Thank you so much for reading *Enable Me, Lord, to Shift*, book #4. If you enjoyed this book, please consider posting a review on Amazon. Even if its' only a few sentences, it would be a huge help. Here is the link to my book page and follow Amazon's steps to post your own review. http://tinyurl.com/y3vpxeyf

A BIG thank you.

Made in the USA
Monee, IL
22 September 2022

13708800R00069